Business Objects SA

By: Terry Sanchez-Clark

Business Objects SA

ISBN: 978-1-60332-023-8

Edited by: Brooke Winger

Copyright© 2008 Equity Press all rights reserved. No part of this publication may be reproduced, stored in a retrieval system, or transmitted in any form or by any means (electronic, mechanical, photocopying, recording or otherwise) without either the prior written permission of the publisher or a license permitting restricted copying in the United States or abroad.

The scanning, uploading and distribution of this book via the internet or via any other means without the permission of the publisher is illegal and punishable by law. Please purchase only authorized electronic editions, and do not participate in or encourage piracy of copyrighted materials.

The programs in this book have been included for instructional value only. They have been tested with care but are not guaranteed for any particular purpose. The publisher does not offer any warranties or representations not does it accept any liabilities with respect to the programs.

Trademarks: All trademarks are the property of their respective owners. Equity Press is not associated with any product or vender mentioned in this book.

Table of Contents

Introduction

France's Business Objects S.A. is a leading provider of software-based enterprise decision support tools to mid-sized and large-scale corporations. Business Objects' client/server software focuses on providing an intuitive "semantic layer" between the end user and the arcane protocols often needed to access corporate databases, data warehouses, and other data repositories. Using their own natural language criteria, Business Objects' clients can perform sophisticated interrogative analysis procedures, producing rapid and specific reports to aid in the decision-making process. By placing the tools to access information in the hands of the end user, Business Objects enables corporations to achieve greater speed and accuracy in decision making and greater competitiveness in the global marketplace.

The company targets four primary market segments. In addition to its principal market of providing front-end support to data warehouses and data marts, the company adds third party decision support services to packaged software applications, such as Microsoft Excel; Internet-based database and data warehouse reporting functionality using the World Wide Web; and decision support services to corporate and third party custom-built relational database management system (RDBMS) applications. Business Objects' client/server software can be adapted for use in corporations ranging from 100 to 10,000 or more licensed stations.

The heart of the company's product line is its Business Objects client/server platform, which entered its version 4.1 in late 1997. Business Object's chief function is to provide a company-patented "semantic layer" meant to shield the end user from the need to formulate data query requests using the highly technical Standard Query Language (SQL) demanded by most data repositories. Instead, a corporation's Information Services department creates a series of graphical "objects" representing SQL search commands, providing the end user with a point-and-click interface tailored to the user's commercial language needs. Objects can be combined to provide highly specific data requests; the results can be presented in graphical charts and diagrams and exported to other decision support software.

Available for use with most major operating systems, including UNIX and Windows, Business Objects is comprised of separate, combinable component modules. Reporter forms the software's core, providing the graphical query engine with which the end user constructs an object-based data request; resulting data is submitted to a report generator, which produces editable, template-based reports, and a graph generator to create a variety of two-dimensional and three-dimensional charts, graphs, and other graphical report tools. An add-on to Reporter is the analysis-oriented Explorer, with which the end user submits the Reporter-generator base report to multidimensional analytic criteria. Reader and Driller function as separate components. Reader enables read-only viewing of previously generated reports; Driller allows users to read and conduct "data mining" analysis on previously generated reports. A fifth component, which began shipping in December 1997, is the company's thin-client, Java applet, Web Intelligence, enabling World Wide Web-based, real-time querying, reporting, and analysis not only within the corporation but also for the corporation clients, suppliers, and partners.

In addition to these core components, Business Objects provides a series of add-on products, including Business Query for Excel, which provides Business Objects querying abilities and reporting directly integrated into that Microsoft application. Business Miner is a Reporter add-on that provides additional "decision tree" graphical formulation for identifying data trends. The company licenses Business Miner from a third party developer. Information Services support is provided by the company's suite of Business Objects environment tools, including Designer; the security and access management module Supervisor; the query request router Document Agent Server; Data Access Drivers for use with major relational database systems; and pre-prepared Rapid Deployment Templates for use with major database applications from SAP, Oracle, Baan, PeopleSoft, and others.

Business Objects XI bridges the gap between the products of the former Crystal Decisions Inc. and the company's classic offerings. What's more, the XI release comes in on time and with several enhancements in addition to its promised back-end integration between Crystal and Business Objects.

Since acquiring Crystal Decisions in 2003, Business Objects has been working to integrate Crystal Reports into its business intelligence suite. Crystal is now part of Business Objects Enterprise XI, but it also continues to be available separately. Crystal Reports XI is no mere re-branding; it's a significant advancement in the Crystal reporting world. Crystal XI has several new features that make it not only easier to author but also to manage and view reports.

CRXI allows you to dive into one of the key new features, dynamic and cascading prompts. Creating these prompts are very easy; but more importantly, it's well documented. Dynamic prompts read their values from a data source and cascading prompts generate their values from the values in other prompts. These features make reports not only easier to build but also easier to maintain because you can update report data without recompiling the report.

Crystal also allows you to store pointers to images in the reports database instead of storing the images themselves, so you no longer have to worry about keeping the images with the reports. You can now preview reports in HTML before publishing them, a significant enhancement for those who have noticed that reports don't always render the same in HTML as in other formats. And finally, Crystal's new drag-and-drop charts allow you to automatically create charts from report data.

The contents of this book are discussions on operating issues surrounding the Business Object XI and Crystal Report XI. The Q & A in this book, mostly concentrated on CRXI (older versions than CRX not included), intends to talk about how developers can add code (from the Formula Editor) to each report section, including code that can change behavior based on input data or even change the look and feel between sections.

BOE XI: General Questions

Question 1: Login can not continue

On a client computer using the Universe Designer to connect to Business Objects Enterprise XI, an error message appears:

"Unable to connect to CMS @@clustername. Login can not continue."

Why does the error message appear and how do you resolve it?

A: The error message appears because the client computer is having problems resolving the name of the Crystal Management Server (CMS).

To fix the name resolution contact your Network Administrator to fix this on a network-wide basis. This is the recommended solution.

To put in place a temporary workaround perform the following steps:

1. Right-click 'Start', click 'Explore', go to \winnt\system32\drivers\etc directory on the client computer.

2. Open the hosts file in a text editor like Notepad.

3. Insert the IP address and CMS server name in the HOSTS file.

The above steps allow the Universe Designer to connect to Business Objects Enterprise XI successfully.

Question 2: Program Object error while running

When scheduling the performance metrics or program objects in the Central Management Console, the following error message appears:

"The Program Object reported an error while running, but no error code was provided"

If –trace is added to command line of the program job server in the Central Configuration Manager, the logs contains the error message:

"trace message: procprogram helper: RExecHelper::Execute() -- Failed to run the command. errno=25";

How can this be fixed?

A: The UNIX system does not have the RSH server running on the system. This issue has been fixed in MHF1. But after applying MHF1, to successfully schedule a performance metric refresh or program object, you also have to change the object settings.

To change the object settings do the following:

1. Log on to CMC.
2. Click Objects > Object Settings button > Program Objects tab.
3. Select the radio button Schedule with the following operating system credentials but do not specify any username or password under it.

For the individual program object, do not specify any username or password on the Process > Logon page.

Question 3: BusObj & Oracle ADI

We just installed BusObj XI and were told that we can't install the application along with Oracle ADI Application Desktop Integration. How do I proceed?

A: If you're running Oracle applications integrator, you should not be running BOEXI on the same server. There are most-likely problems between the ways both systems handle similar tasks. If Business Objects is telling you that their software won't work in tandem with ADI, I would definitely heed to their advice. Worst-case scenario, you'd cause irreparable damage to your ADI installation. Best case scenario, both applications are competing for system resources.

Question 4: Determine which report is running

Is there a way to determine which reports are currently running?

A: Here is the URL entry you would put into your browser address:
https://<server>/businessobjects/enterprise115/WebTools/web samples/query/logonform.aspx?framework=&page=current

Once you hit this site you'll be prompted for the administrator credentials. After passing through the login formalities you'll be presented with an open area where you can type:

"select SI_ID,SI_NAME, SI_DESCRIPTION from CI_INFOOBJECTS where SI_SCHEDULE_STATUS = 0"

You can select whatever you like, you can include the Object ID, name and whatever description is available. Run that via Query Builder or build an application that utilizes the SDK and run it in that manner.

Question 5: Input file repository location change

My Input File Repository is located in the standard Program Files\Business Objects\BusinessObjects Enterprise 11.5. I initially installed and I placed it on the C: drive which has a limited space.

Is it possible to move parts of this to another drive and then change a setting somewhere to reflect the changes?

A: During the process of installing BOE XI, there are no provisions for establishing the Input/Output FRS to an alternate location; however, this can be done prior to installation. Here are the steps:

1. Establish a folder on the alternate location (i.e. D:\FileStore), then under d:\filestore establish three more sub-folders (Input, Output, Temp).

2. Go to the CMC and download all the processes.

3. Locate the original file store folder and copy items over to new area (ref step 1).

4. Go to the CMC: (http://<server>/businessobjects/enterprise115/admin/en/admin.cwr), login as administrator then go to Servers and locate the "Input.xxx" entry, click on it, and change the entry for root directory accordingly. Do likewise for the "Output.xxx" entry. Go back to the CCM and up all services.

Take note that the alternate location mentioned in step #1 can also be a UNC versus a local drive; however, when using a UNC, you will need to have administrative rights to the drive on the network. There are additional security impacts to consider when choosing this option.

Question 6: E-mail only when report contains data

I need to have a scheduled/run report only be e-mailed to users if it actually contains data. I thought perhaps I could use an event but I have no idea where to begin.

What are the possible steps to do this?

A: Try the following steps:

1. Schedule the report to some destination (folder).

2. Check files size using a batch file (there are scripts you can find online).

3. Once size is good (need trial and error to come up with a size number), batch file should copy that file to some folder, which could trigger the instance of a report to run with email destination.

Batch file can be scheduled on server or perhaps within BOXI. You also need to create a file based event.

Question 7: Pass ID field in list of values

I have a table with three columns like this

ID Name Salary
1 Siva 100
2 Raja 50
3 Raja 40

I have prompted the users to select the name from the list of values.
Users can see the List of Names like this:
Siva(1)
Raja(2)

Raja(3)

I want to pass the ID field when they select name to the database. How can I pass ID field instead of Name?

A: When populating the pick list for the parameter you can select use description (it allows name, description or both) for the display and then the users will see the name. Since you have used the id field, you can reference it in the record selection.

Question 8: Find jobs that are running now

How do I find a list of jobs that are running right now?

It tells me 4 jobs are running in CMC>Settings>Metrics and I want to find out which are these jobs, who submitted them, etc.

A: Open the XI launch pad and click at "Instance Manager" under Administration tools in the left side frame. Log into to this application and you will see the drop down which will give you the information you need.

Question 9: ODBC selection

Is it also possible for users when viewing a report through info view, be given the option to select an ODBC connection for the report they are trying to use? We want our users to select the database on the server which they want to run the report against.

A: You should use Business Views to allow users the option to select the data source through Info view. Business Views are one of the semantic layers available to BOE XI along with Universes. Business Views allow you to set up something called a Dynamic Data Connection. This allows you to dynamically change from one database to another dependent on a report parameter.

Question 10: Hiding Group Tree

I have reports that are viewed from infoview but group tree shows up.

How will I hide the “Group Tree” in Business Objects Enterprise XI?

A: The only way this can be done is to open each report. Select "Report Options", clear the check box from "Create Group Tree" and save back to Enterprise.

The information for configuring BO Enterprise XI .Net to disable the "Group Tree" is as follows:

You need to configure the web.config on the box that has the Web Component Adapter (WCA).

To configure the .NET WCA, you need to edit the web.config file associated with the WCA.

This file is located in the following directory:
C:\Program Files\Business Objects\BusinessObjects Enterprise11\Web\ Content\application

To configure web.config

1. Stop your application server.
2. Edit the web.config file by using a text editor such as Notepad.

   The following entry will disable the "Group Tree"
   <context-param>
   <param-name>viewrpt.groupTreeGenerate</param-name>
   <param-value>false</param-value>
   <description>”true” or “false” value determining whether a group tree will be generated.</description>
   </context-param>

3. Restart your application server.

If you have more than one system with a WCA you must edit each of the files.

For the JAVA WCA the process is as follows:

1. Stop your application server.
2. Extract the web.xml file from the webcompadapter.war archive.
3. Edit the file by using a text editor such as Notepad or vi.
4. Reinsert the file into the WEB-INF directory in webcompadapter.war. To reinsert web.xml into WEB-INF using WinZip, right-click on the WEB-INF directory that contains your edited web.xml file and select "Add to Zip File...". Adding the file in this way ensures that it is placed in the correct directory inside the archive.
5. Restart your application server.

For the .NET, you have to set the value of key="viewrpt.groupTreeHide" to True and value of key="viewrpt.groupTreeGenerate" to False in the c:\program files\Business Objects BusinessObjects Enterprise11\Webcontent\ web.config file.

Question 11: Viewer Hyperlink from Infoview error

We are running BOE XI on a Windows Server 2003 box using IIS 6.0. The clients are all using Windows XP.

I have successfully used the hyperlink (Add place holder) in the "send to email" destination in 'Infoview' to have an instance of a report mailed to users. We also use SSO. However, after a recent update (latest BOXI and Common XI update) the links no longer work. On clicking a link, the browser returns: "An error has occurred: An unknown error has occurred."

Is there a known solution to this?

A: Here is the source of original openDocument.aspx. We had a similar problem and noticed that my openDocument.aspx was corrupted. Make a backup CPU and paste the following code in openDocument.aspx and see if it helps.

```
<%@ LANGUAGE="JSCRIPT" CODEPAGE=65001 %>
<%
Response.Expires = -1;
Response.ContentType = "text/html";
Response.Charset = "UTF-8";
%>
<!--#include file="tools/utils.aspx" -->
<%
var bFindCharset = true;      //false: no guessing is
done with charset for the incoming query string, use
the one defined by sCharset variable
                //true: will try to read an optional
parameter &charset= to determine charset encoding
var sForceCharset = "UTF-8";     //charset by default,
change this to support legacy OpenDocument URLs not
url-encoded with UTF-8
                //empty string "" would mean to use
the default charset on this platform
var sCharset = new String(sForceCharset);
if (bFindCharset) {
    var        sCharsetTemp        =        ""        +
Request.QueryString("charset");
```

```
    if (sCharsetTemp != "undefined") {      //if the
param exists it MUST have a valid charset name value,
otherwise the behavior is not certain...
        sCharset = sCharsetTemp;
        }
    }

//switch to the corresponding codepage for reading
query string parameters
//currently only a limited number of codepage is
supported...
if (sCharset.toLowerCase() == "iso-8859-1")
Session.CodePage = 1252;
else if (sCharset.toLowerCase() == "shift-jis")
Session.CodePage = 932;
else if (sCharset.toLowerCase() == "iso-2022-kr")
Session.CodePage = 949;
else if (sCharset.toLowerCase() == "gb2312")
Session.CodePage = 936;
else if (sCharset.toLowerCase() == "big5")
Session.CodePage = 950;
else Session.CodePage = 65001;

//openDocument.asp
//see spec bluecanal
///////////////////////////////////////////////////////
//////////////////////////
//Description :
//Properties :
///////////////////////////////////////////////////////
//////////////////////////
```

/* Here is the exhaustive list of supported query string parameter as defined in latest spec (CBo)

```
* sRepoType (legacy: RepoType)
 * sRepo (specific CBO)
 * sPath (specific CBO)
 * sDocName (legacy: sDoc)
 * sAlternateDocName (specific CBO)
 * sType (legacy: sTyp, legacy values: "W"qy, "R"ep,
"B"qy)
 * sIDType (specific CBO, can be CUID, GUID, RUID,
ParentID, InfoObjectID (default))
 * iDocID
 * sReportName (legacy: sReport ?)
 * sPartContext (specific CBO)
 * sReportPart (specific CBO)
 * sReportMode
```

```
 * sInstance (specific CB0)
 * lsM*, lsR*, lsS* and lsC*
 * sRefresh (legacy: Refresh, sForceRefresh)
 * NAII
 * sOutputFormat
 * sViewer
 * sWindow
 * sMode
 * Page (only legacy ?)
 * sKind (specific CB1)
 * token
 * sf
 * buttonrefresh
 * buttonexport
 * buttonprint
 *
 */

/*
//From this list we define an array containing all
authorized parameters.
//We removed the implicit parameters passed to IV
(docname, id, repotype, doctype)
//and the parameter already handled by this page's
logic (ls* for prompts and sRefresh)
var stAutorizedParams = new Array(
//     "sRepoType", "RepoType",
     "sRepo",
     "sPath",
//     "sDocName", "sDoc",
     "sAlternateDocName",
//     "sType", "sTyp",
//     "sIDType",     // now the ID type for crystal is
stored inside the id
//     "iDocID",
     "sReportName", "sReport",
     "sPartContext",
     "sReportPart",
     "sReportMode",
     "sInstance",
//     "lsM*", "lsR*", "lsS*", "lsC*",
//     "sRefresh", "Refresh", "sForceRefresh",
     "NAII",
     "sOutputFormat",
     "sViewer",
     "sWindow",      // is handled here but passed to
viewer anyway (in case of the viewer wants to know it
is opened in a window)
```

```
    "sMode",
//     "sEntry",     // for future usage
//     "sKind",
//     "token",
    "Page",
    "sf",
    "buttonrefresh",
    "buttonexport",
    "buttonprint"
    );
*/

var stHandledParams = new Array(
    "sRepoType", "RepoType",
    "sDocName", "sDoc",
    "sType", "sTyp",
    "sIDType",      // now the ID type for crystal is
stored inside the id
    "iDocID",
    "lsM*", "lsR*", "lsS*", "lsC*",
    "sRefresh", "Refresh", "sForceRefresh",
    "sEntry",    // for future usage
    "sKind",
    "token"
    );

//get the corresponding hashtable for faster lookup
(+lowercase keys)
var          htHandledParams             =         new
Array(stHandledParams.length);
for (var ii = 0 ; ii < stHandledParams.length ; ii++)
{

htHandledParams[stHandledParams[ii].toLowerCase()]  =
"Y";
    }

//get parameters
var sDocName = "" + Request.QueryString("sDoc");
if(sDocName    ==    "undefined"    ||    sDocName    ==    "")
sDocName = "" + Request.QueryString("sDocName");
if(sDocName    ==    "undefined"    ||    sDocName    ==    "")
sDocName = "untitled";

//special CBO, Crystal uses different ID types. Read
this value here
var sIDType = "" + Request.QueryString("sIDType"); if
(sIDType == "undefined") sIDType = "";
sIDType = sIDType.toLowerCase();
```

```
var sDocID   = "" + Request.QueryString("iDocID");
if(sDocID == "undefined" || sDocID == "") sDocID =
"0"; //default
var iDocID = 0;
if (sIDType != "cuid"
 && sIDType != "guid"
 && sIDType != "ruid"
 && sIDType != "parentid"
 && strIsNumeric(sDocID)) {        //this is not a
crystal special ID type, but a normal numeric ID (BO
or InfoObjectID)
    iDocID = sDocID - 0;
    sDocID = "" + iDocID;
    }

var sDocType = "" + Request.QueryString("sType");
if(sDocType == "undefined" || sDocType == "")
sDocType = "" + Request.QueryString("sTyp");
if(sDocType == "undefined" || sDocType == "")
sDocType = "" + Request.QueryString("sDocType");

//check parameter type
if(sDocType == "W") sDocType = "wqy";
else if(sDocType == "R") sDocType = "rep";
else if(sDocType == "B")  sDocType = "bqy";

//not used but here for consistancy
var         documentDomain         =         ""         +
Request.QueryString("sRepo");
if(documentDomain == "undefined" || documentDomain ==
"") documentDomain = "Document";

var    documentRepoType                    =    ""    +
Request.QueryString("RepoType");
if(documentRepoType        ==        "undefined"       ||
documentRepoType   ==   "")   documentRepoType   =   ""   +
Request.QueryString("sRepoType");
if(documentRepoType        ==        "undefined"       ||
documentRepoType == "") documentRepoType = "0";

var iDocRepoType = "0";
//not sure if the repo is C,M,I or corporate etc
if(documentRepoType == "Inbox" || documentRepoType ==
"inbox"    ||    documentRepoType    ==    "I"    ||
documentRepoType == "1")
    documentRepoType = "1";
```

```
else    if(documentRepoType    ==    "personal"    ||
documentRepoType == "Personal" || documentRepoType ==
"M" || documentRepoType == "2")
    documentRepoType = "2";

//we use the sIDType param to know what kind of ID is
the resource
//the documentRepoType will depend on that:
//CUID, GUID, RUID or ParentID => documentRepoType =
"10"
//others    (unspecified    or    InfoObjectID)    =>
documentRepoType = "0", assimiled to a BOBJ corporate
resource
if (    sIDType == "cuid" ||
    sIDType == "guid" ||
    sIDType == "ruid" ||
    sIDType == "parentid") {
    documentRepoType = "10";        //special faked
repotype for this type of resource
    sDocID = sIDType + "," + sDocID;    //a composite
ID to remind ID type: <sIDType>,<sDocID>. Will be
parsed by crystal viewers
    }

else documentRepoType = "0";

//other values can go here

//These I am not sure of
//var    documentReport                =    ""    +
Request.QueryString("Report");
//var    documentPage                  =    ""    +
Request.QueryString("Page");
//var    documentHide                  =    ""    +
Request.QueryString("Hide");

//refresh
var bRefresh = false;
var sRefresh = "" + Request.QueryString("Refresh");
if(sRefresh  ==  "undefined"  ||  sRefresh  ==  "")
sRefresh = "" + Request.QueryString("sRefresh");
if(sRefresh  ==  "undefined"  ||  sRefresh  ==  "")
sRefresh = "" + Request.QueryString("sForceRefresh");

if(sRefresh  !=  "undefined"  ||  sRefresh  !=  "")
bRefresh = (sRefresh == "Y" || sRefresh == "yes")?
true : false;

var sDocToken      = "";      //null presumably
```

```
var sKind = "" + Request.QueryString("sKind");
var token = "" + Request.QueryString("token");

/*
open doc with prompts feature:
- check for lsS or lsM
- we do this here and then encode the URL
- the prompts need to be regathered at the viewer end
using the same technique
*/
//===============PROMPT
GATHERING========================//
//var hasNAII = false;
var prompts = "";
var sOtherParams = "";
var e = Request.QueryString.GetEnumerator();
while( e.MoveNext() )
{
    var name = "" + e.Current;
    var params = Request.QueryString.GetValues(name);
    if          ((name.indexOf("lsS")==0)           ||
(name.indexOf("lsM")==0) || (name.indexOf("lsC")==0))
    {
        if (prompts != "") prompts += "&";     //add &
for correct url
        if (sDocType == "wid")
        {    //wid use a ; seperated list
            prompts +=  URLEncodeUTF8(name)  +  "=";
//convert to ; seperated list
            for (var i = 0; i < params.length; i++)
            {
                //Must encode ; character to get the
whole QueryString encoded
                prompts      +=      (i      >      0      ?
URLEncodeUTF8(";") : "") + URLEncodeUTF8(params[i]);
            }
        }
        else
        {
            for (var i = 0; i < params.length; i++)
            {
                prompts  +=  (i  >  0  ?  "&"  :  "")  +
URLEncodeUTF8(name) + "=" + URLEncodeUTF8(params[i]);
            }
        }
    }
/*
    else if (name.indexOf("NAII") > -1)
```

```
    {
        hasNAII = true; //related to prompts only,
has no value
    }
*/
    else if (name.indexOf("lsR")==0) {     //added for
CB0, range prompt (eg: &lsRCity=[Austin..Chicago])
        prompts += (prompts != "" ? "&" : "") +
URLEncodeUTF8(name)          +          "="          +
URLEncodeUTF8(""+Request.QueryString(name));
        }
    else                                              if
(typeof(htHandledParams[name.toLowerCase()])          ==
"undefined") {    //don't pass already handled params
        sOtherParams += (sOtherParams != "" ? "&" :
"")     +     URLEncodeUTF8(name)     +     "="     +
URLEncodeUTF8(""+Request.QueryString(name));
        }
}//eof enumeration

//build the uid in the infoview style:
//uid         is         under         the         form
<name>,<id>,<repotype>,<doctype>,<SDK  token>.  Ex  :
"3Reports_2onlyhavesections,39614,0,rep,"
var sDocUID = sDocName + C_SEP + sDocID + C_SEP +
documentRepoType  +  C_SEP  +  sDocType  +  C_SEP  +
sDocToken + C_SEP + sKind;

//cmdP1 = the docuid
var   sRespURL   =   "documentXML.aspx?token="   +
URLEncodeUTF8(token)        +        "&cmdP1="        +
URLEncodeUTF8(sDocUID);

//cmdP2 has the prompts and other parameters
var cmdP2 = prompts /* + (hasNAII ? "&NAII=" : "")
*/;    //URL chunk for prompts and NAII
if (sOtherParams != "" && cmdP2 != "") cmdP2 += "&";
cmdP2 += sOtherParams;

//cmdP2 can be used for the extra parameter values
like prompts, report and page
//NB: a new type of URL redirection can now be
specified using askPromptView for cmd
if (prompts != "")
{
    sRespURL                                          +=
"&cmd=askPromptView&cmdBlock=all&cmdP2="              +
URLEncodeUTF8(cmdP2);
}
else
```

```
{
    if(bRefresh)
    {
        sRespURL                                        +=
"&cmd=askView&cmdBlock=all&cmdP2="                       +
URLEncodeUTF8((cmdP2 == "" ? "" : (cmdP2 + "&")) +
"sRefresh=yes&refresh=Y");
    }
    else
    {
        sRespURL                                        +=
"&cmd=askView&cmdBlock=all&cmdP2="                       +
URLEncodeUTF8(cmdP2);    //need   cmdP2   for   other
parameters
    }
}
//saves the real document URL into HTTP session, in
case we have to login
Session("extRedirectionURL") = sRespURL;

Session.CodePage = 65001;    //re-set the codepage to
UTF8 for writing this page result
%>
<HTML>
<HEAD>
<META  HTTP-EQUIV="Content-Type"  CONTENT="text/html;
charset=UTF-8">
</HEAD>
%>
}
</SCRIPT>
<BODY onload='findParent();'></BODY>
</HTML>
<SCRIPT language='javascript1.3'>
function  MM_openBrWindow(theURL,  winName,  features,
bUnique) {
    var _winName = winName;
    if (!bUnique) {
        var dtemp = new Date();
        _winName = _winName + dtemp.getTime();
        }
    pop = window.open(theURL, _winName, features);
    pop.opener = self;
}

function            getQueryParamValue(strQueryString,
strParamName) {
    var strRet = "";
```

```
    if("undefined"    !=    typeof(strQueryString)    &&
strQueryString != null) {
        var                arrQueryParam                =
strQueryString.split('&');
        for (var i=0;i<arrQueryParam.length;i++) {
            var strName = arrQueryParam[i];
            var strValue = "";
            var iPos = arrQueryParam[i].indexOf('=');
            if (iPos>=0) {
                strName                                 =
arrQueryParam[i].substring(0, iPos);
                strValue                                =
arrQueryParam[i].substring(iPos + 1);
            }
            if (strParamName == strName) {
                strRet = strValue;
                break;
            }
        }
    }
    return strRet;
}

function findParent() {
<%
var sWindow      = Request.QueryString("sWindow"); if
(sWindow == null) sWindow = "Same";
var bNewWin = false;
if (sWindow != "Same") {
    bNewWin = true;
    //if sWindow  != New then the provided string is
the identifier of the new window
    }

if (bNewWin) {
    %>
    MM_openBrWindow('<%=sRespURL   %>',    '<%=sWindow
%>',  '',  <%=(sWindow  ==  "New"  ?  "false"  :  "true")
%>);
//toolbar=yes,location=yes,status=yes,resizable=yes,w
idth=' + width + ',height=' + height, false);
    history.back();
    <%
    }
else {
    %>
    /*
    var found = false;
    var frameToFind = "XML.aspx";
    var obj = window;
```

```
    try {
        while  (!found  &&  typeof(obj.parent)  !=
"undefined" && obj.parent != obj) {     //escape
clause please
            var      loc      =      ""      +
obj.parent.document.location;
            if (loc.indexOf(frameToFind) < 0) {
                obj = obj.parent;
                }
            else {
                found = true;
                }
            }
        }
    catch(e) {    //cross domain issue ? assume that
this URL is like an external one
        found = false;
        }

    //if test needed
    if (found) {    //open in parent ie documentXML
or myInfoviewXML frame level
        obj = obj.parent;
        if                   ((""                +
obj.document.location.href).indexOf("documentXML.aspx
") > 0) {
            //we are in documentXML frameset, let's
stack the current documentXML URL (including possibly
new token)
            //to allow backward navigation (close)
history
            //we ask the action header bar the real
UID of the (previously) opened doc
            if      (typeof(obj.parent.push)      !=
"undefined" && typeof(obj.getDocUID) != "undefined")
{   //the stack should be defined in webiHome.jsp
                //calculate the URL, knowing the
current docUID, and asking viewer for the last
storage token
                var curDocUID = obj.getDocUID();
                var              sURL              =
"documentXML.aspx?ctxLayout_last=fromSession&cmdBlock
=all&cmd=askView&cmdP1=" + URLEncodeUTF8(curDocUID);
//here is the real URL to come back to the currently
opened document
                obj.parent.push(sURL, obj.timeStamp);
//push this URL into the stack, and stamp it to help
manage browser's back/forward
```

```
                    }
                }
            if      (typeof(obj.asyncOpenDocument)       !=
"undefined") {
                var bIE = (document.all ? true : false);
                var              sViewerURL                =
obj.frames[1].location.href;
                var              sViewType                 =
getQueryParamValue(sViewerURL, "ViewType") ;
                obj.asyncOpenDocument('<%=sRespURL%>');
//asynchronous launch of URL
                if   (!bIE   ||   sViewType   !=   "P")   {
//Don't do back if the document is wid or rep and
viewed on PDF on IE
                                 //FR  103137,  apparently
acroread on IE is already doing this...
                    history.back();
                    }
                }
            else        obj.document.location.href        =
'<%=sRespURL%>';
            }
        else {     //this should handle the external URL
case ...
            //document.location.href     =     '<%="/"    +
Application("wiroot")                                 +
"/scripts/login/topStart.html"%>';
            document.location.replace('<%="/"             +
Application("wiroot")                                 +
"/scripts/login/topStart.html"%>');
            }
        */
        var mywin = window;
        while (mywin != mywin.parent && mywin.parent &&
(mywin.name     ==     'ceframe'     ||     mywin.name     ==
'documentFrame000hb')) {
            mywin = mywin.parent;
        }
        mywin.document.location.replace("<%=sRespURL%>");
        <%
        }
```

Question 12: Info Viewer Issue

I can log onto the InfoView, view and schedule reports with no problem. However, I have created 2 other users and they both get this error when they try to view a report instance:

"There are no page servers connected to the cache server or all connected Page Servers are disabled or all connected Page Servers are not part of the specified server group. Please try to reconnect later."

They can successfully schedule reports but cannot view them. One of the users has Admin access and can successfully use CMS and save/schedule all reports he has written but cannot view a single one via the infoview portal.

A: Change their viewer preference to "Advanced DHTML viewer" in InfoView. Your cache or page servers are down (or disabled). If you activate them, your users can use any viewer.

Question 13: Field length changes from CR XI view to BO XI InfoView

I have some database fields on my report that are purposely made smaller to only display first part of field due to space constraints. The fields display correctly on my PC with CR XI. When I move the reports to BOE XI on our Solaris machine and view through InfoView, the field displays the entire field and overlaps the next field.

How can I correct this?

A: Format the field and select the "Can Grow" option and set it to 1 line max. This will truncate the field to whatever width is there.

Question 14: Tool to get type of info

I want to know who is using our Business Objects XI Release 2 system. Specifically I want to know things like how regularly users are running reports or even how frequently theya re using the system at all. I know that we could probably write queries off of the system database.

Is there any documentation on the schema?

A: Version XI comes with a suite of auditing reports that will tell you what you want to know regarding system usage.

In the X:\Program Files\Business Objects\BusinessObjects Enterprise 11.5\Samples folder where X is your install drive, is the file called auditing_rpt_en.biar.

This BIAR file contains the suite of auditing reports and the audit universe that the reports utilize.

To access the sample auditing reports, you need to import them from the sample auditing reports Business Intelligence Archive Resource (BIAR) file.

1. Use the Import Wizard located in the BusinessObjects XI Release 2 Start menu program group to import the sample auditing reports BIAR file.

2. Specify the BIAR file as the source and provide the following path to the BIAR file:

<Installation directory>\Business Objects\BusinessObjects Enterprise 11.5\Samples\auditing_rpt_en.biar

3. Specify your Content Management Server (CMS) as the destination and proceed with the import.

Upon completion of the import, the sample auditing report will be located in the Auditor folder in the top level folders. These reports use the Audit universe and to get the reports working you may need to open the universe and create a new data connection to the audit database in order to get the reports to work.

The option to turn on auditing, the Audit universe and reports are only available if you have Premium licensing. If you're on Professional licenses where users will only access Crystal, then auditing is not an option.

In order to turn on auditing and select the actions to be audited, you have to log into the CMC, select servers, and turn on auditing for specific servers. On the cache server, turn on "A report has been viewed successfully" to show who is viewing reports - both on-demand and instances. On the Report Job Server, turn on "A job has been run successfully" to see who is scheduling instances. If your users use the Advanced DHTML Viewer, you'll also need to turn on several options on the RAS.

Also, if you don't have the auditing feature, you should be able to get some of this information through the SDK. You won't be able to see who is viewing reports on demand, but you should be able to see who is scheduling instances of reports and when a user last logged in.

Question 15: Managing Dynamic Parameter BVs

We are using a BOE-XI (R2) patched with SP-1, MHF-1 and CHF-15.

We have some RPT developers who are now starting to do some testing of the "Dynamic Parameter" functions in Crystal Reports XI.

When these reports are posted to our BOE-XI (R2) infrastructure they create Business Views components that need to be configured by an Admin for database connection through the desktop "Business View Manager" tool.

This process is a little odd in comparison to managing RPTs or WebI documents which left us with the following questions:

1. Is there any way to manage these Business Views for RPT Dynamic Parameters via the CMC rather than the desktop BV Manager tool?
2. If we update/publish RPTs with Business Views to the BOE-XI (R2) infrastructure, are existing BVs updated or new BVs created?
3. How can we determine which specific Business Views are tied to which specific RPTs on our BOE-XI (R2) infrastructure?
4. Can Business View lists be scheduled to update at a certain time each day (like List-Of-Values) rather than execute the SQL each time the drop-down is clicked in InfoView?
5. Are there any documents for managing Dynamic Parameter Business Views in BOE-XI (R2)?

A: The answers to your queries are as follows:

1. No, the only way to manage the BV's is to use the Business View Manager.

2. Once you publish the report the first time, a new BV is created in Enterprise. If you republish the report that was already published in Enterprise, it will use the existing BV.

3. You have to open the report file and look at the name of the LOV it is using. You may be able to get the folder name from here to determine what folder the BV is stored in.

4. The LOV object that is created off of the BV for the parameter can be scheduled. Right click on the LOV object in the BV manager's Repository Explorer and you will see an option to schedule it.

5. Always create the BV objects you need for parameters in the BV Manager and then point the report to the appropriate LOV object. This will make it easier to organize and maintain the objects rather than letting duplicate objects get created when users publish reports.

   Remove the rights to the folder that Crystal will publish and create the BV's in when a report is published. This will prevent a user from being able to create new BV's without the administrator knowing about it.

Question 16: Printing very slow from Java viewer

On a multi-page report from a Java viewer, it will print about 1 page per minute instead of all at once. It doesn't send all the pages to the printer.

What adjustments should I make?

A: When viewing the report, go to the last page then print. The viewers are essentially page-on-demand, so by going to the last page, you force it to retrieve all the data from the database before having it sent to the printer. Database access is the slowest part of report activity.

Another trick is to place the "totalpagecount" on the first page; this forces Crystal to run the entire report to determine how many pages there are.

So a formula of:

"Page: " & totext(pagenumber,0,"") &" of " & totext(totalpagecount ,0,"")

In the page footer should net the same results, only you won't need to go to the last page prior to printing.

Question 17: Auditing database

Does the auditing database have to be different from the CMS database?

A: Yes, it can be on the same physical database server but it is a totally different set of tables in a different database schema.

Name your database schemas with something clear so as to avoid confusion like:

BOEXI_R2_PROD_AUDIT
BOEXI_R2_PROD_CMS

BOEXI_R2_DEV_AUDIT
BOEXI_R2_DEV_CMS

Depending on your volume of traffic, the size/number of BOE-XI services/processes you intend to audit and the type of database you are using (e.g. MySQL vs. ORACLE 10G), you might want to put them on different physical database servers if it's a very large BOE-XI install.

A brand new audit database with no history is in the order of 5MB. Quite small.

Typically 512MB to 1024 MB is sufficient for an ongoing Audit database depending on system size and usage.

As BO support suggests, the long term size of the audit database is dependent upon how many items you set BOE to Audit, on how many users are on your system and on how many reports are run by your system.

The other thing to remember about auditing in BOE XI is that the log files are written to a temporary file prior to being uploaded to the audit database. These temporary files are created on the default drive and default to a five minute lifespan. After five minutes these files are purged and uploaded to the audit database. An independent log file is kept for each BOE Server that you invoke the auditing facility for.

Question 18: Error when viewing report in InfoView

When attempting to view a report in InfoView, the following error message appears: "An error has occurred: No 508 compliant...found in resource strings";

What is causing this error? How do I resolve this issue?

A: This message occurs because the business objects virtual directory in Internet Information Server (IIS) is set to use 2.0 version of the .NET framework. Business Objects Enterprise XI only supports version 1.1 of the .NET framework.

To resolve this error message do the following:

1. Go to Start > Settings > Control Panel > Administrative Tools > Internet Services Manager.
2. Expand the objects tree for the IIS Server > Web Sites > Default Web Site.
3. Right-click the businessobjects virtual directory and choose Properties from the context menu.
4. Select the ASP.NET tab.
5. Using the drop down box change the version from 2.0.50727 to 1.1.4322. Note your point versions may not match these exactly; the essential version is 1.1x and not 2.x.
6. Click the OK button to save your changes.
7. Repeat steps 3 through 6 for the crystalreportviewers11 virtual directory.
8. Click Start, click Run, and type "iisreset" to shut down and restart IIS.

If the virtual directory version of the ASP.NET framework and your Internet Information Server does not list version 1.1x then do the following:

1. Uninstall version 2.0 of the .NET Framework
2. Reinstall version 1.1.
3. To install version 2.0 of the .NET Framework in a side-by-side configuration without updating ASP .NET click Start, click Run and use the following switches:

   dotnetfx.exe /c:"install /noaspupgrade /l /q"

Question 19: Edit ASPX file

I'm using BOEXI / MSSQL2K / Windows 2003 Advanced Server.

We're using InfoView to deploy and execute reports. When a user schedules a report, they see the options to change the database Logon.

Is there a way to hide that option?

A: You can fairly easily edit the JSP or ASPX file to comment out the section that requests the database information.

You need to edit this file:
c:\Program Files\Business Objects\BusinessObjects Enterprise 11.5\Web Content\Enterprise115\InfoView\Report\report_scheduleBody.aspx

and comment out this:

```
<!--
<tr id="dBLogonLinksPanel" runat="server">
<td width="1"><asp:linkbutton id="dBLogonImgLink" CssClass="appTreeCtrl" Runat="server" CausesValidation="True">
<asp:Image CssClass="appTreeCtrl" id="dBLogonImg" ImageUrl="../images/minus.gif" border="0" runat="server" ImageAlign="middle" AlternateText=""></asp:Image>
</asp:linkbutton></td>
<td class="schedule" width='99%'><asp:linkbutton id="dBLogonLabelLink" runat="server" CssClass="appTreeCtrl" CausesValidation="True"
Font-Bold="True"></asp:linkbutton></td>
</tr>

<tr id="dBLogonPanel" runat="server">
<td> </td>
```

```
                    <td class="schedule">
                        <!--#include
virtual="report_scheduleBody_include_db.aspx"--></td>
                </tr>
                -->
```

We commented out the filters, printers, server groups, and events panels so that our users only see the options that they really need to use. These are all on the same page, just note that there are two <tr>s for each option and you need to comment out both of them. The first one will start <tr id="XXXXXLinksPanel" and the second one will start <tr id="XXXXXPanel". Comment out both of these and the section will disappear.

Question 20: Schedule Dynamic Parameters in RPTs

A user has created a CR-XI (R2) Report file that has a dynamic parameter which pulls from an Oracle 9i database.

It works fine on the DESKTOP from CR-XI (R2) but when published into BOE-XI (R2), the report asks for a database login when the user tries to enter the parameter while scheduling a report. This doesn't happen when viewing the report but only when scheduling.

What is happening here? Is there a fix to this?

A: When you post a report using a dynamic parameter, you also need to save the database password in Business View Manager; it will not use the db username/password from the CMC. See this KB article for instructions on how to save the password in Business View Manager:

When you create a dynamic parameter in Crystal Reports, the components of a Business View are created for you in Business View Manager. When the data connection is created in Business View Manager, it does not contain database logon information by default, so this information needs to be provided.

To not get prompted when changing the parameter value, use the following steps:

1. Launch Business View Manager and close the default screen that appears.
2. Go to the 'View' menu and click 'Repository Explorer'.
3. Expand the Dynamic Cascading Prompts folder and find your Data Connection for your dynamic parameter (it will have the name of the parameter and then '_DC').
4. Double-click the Data Connection.

5. On the left hand side, you should see three fields: 'User Name', 'Password' and 'Runtime Prompt'.

6. Type your database user name and password and then set 'Runtime Prompt' to 'Never Prompt'.

7. Save the changes to the Data Connection.

Upon completing these steps, you will not be prompted for database logon information when changing parameter values.

You can also schedule the LOV's to run at whatever frequency that you want so that they don't have to refresh when the report is viewed. You can do this through the BV Manager, and then opening up the Repository Explorer, locating the LOV object and then right clicking the LOV object and choosing schedule.

Question 21: Hiding the Navigation Tree in BOExir2

When a report is viewed in BOExir2 it shows navigation tree.

How do I turn that default off? I would rather have the viewer page be taken up by the report, and for the user to select the hide/ show navigation tree if required.

A: You can either set the Report Option "Create Group Tree" to off in each report inside of Crystal Reports XI or you can modify the Web Component adaptor code like this:

(This is an excerpt from the Business Objects XI Release 2 Deployment manual and is called xir2_bip_deploy_en.pdf)

To configure the Java WCA you edit the web.xml file associated with the
WCA:
• Windows: C:\Program Files\Business Objects\BusinessObjects Enterprise 11.5\java\applications directory
• UNIX: WEB-INF subdirectory of the webcompadapter.war archive file
stored in the bobje_root/enterprise115/java/applications directory
For example, the context parameter that controls whether a group tree will be
generated looks like this:

```
<context-param>
<param-name>viewrpt.groupTreeGenerate</param-name>
<param-value>true</param-value>
<desctiption>"true" or "false" value determining whether
a group tree will be generated.</description>
</context-param>
```

To change the value of a context parameter, edit the value between the
<param-value> </param-value> tags.

CRYSTAL REPORT: Charts and Graphs

Question 22: Drilldown graphs

Using Crystal Reports 11, I'm trying to create a drill down pie chart. Not sure why this particular report won't allow for that but I can't get seem to enable the drill down feature.

In this particular report, I just display some detail, sum up four values and generate a pie chart of those four summed values. Ex: sum of 0 to 30, sum of 30 to 60, sum of 60 to 90, and sum of > 90 days. The pie chart works fine and simply shows the number of records for each of the four summed values mentioned above, however it's not allowing for drill down.

I'm able to select the "group" button in the chart now but obviously doing something wrong. I have the four ranges (formulas) but can only select one of them. I want the pie chart to show the four formulas or ranges, which it does, however I want to be able to click on any of the four and drill down to that particular detail. How can I do this?

A: Your group has to be based on a formula that returns the various ranges. You are trying to cluster by summary values and to do this; you will need to create a command that returns the summary value, e.g.

```
Select
(select sum(a.`qty`) from table a where
a.`ID` = table.`ID`) as sumx, table.`ID`, table.`qty`,
table.`otherfield`
from table
```

...where ID represents the field within which you are summing the qty.

Place the desired fields in the detail section. Then insert a group in the main report on this formula {@grp}:

```
if {command.sumx} <= 30 then "0 to 30" else
if {command.sumx} <= 60 then "31 to 60" else
if {command.sumx} <= 90 then "61 to 90" else
if {command.sumx} > 90 then "90+"
```

Insert a maximum on {command.sumx} at the {@grp} level in order to activate the group option for the chart. Then choose {@grp} as the on change of field, and maximum of {command.sumx} as the show value field.

Question 23: Charting subgroup data

I want to create a chart off this report data:

T3a - Credits achieved at each credit level by Gender

Year	Gender	Levels 1-2	Level 3	Level 4	Levels 5 - 8	Total
2003	Female	5382	11160	4779	1484	22805
	Male	34493	47761	22496	7416	112166
	Total	39875	58921	27275	8900	134971
2004	Female	14501	11344	8556	1467	35868
	Male	56327	59856	34119	3660	153962
	Total	70828	71200	42675	5127	189830
2005	Female	24406	11519	13823	2183	51931
	Male	68870	54965	38181	4213	166229
	Total	93276	66484	52004	6396	218160
2006	Female	49908	11777	6915	1380	69980
	Male	144223	65652	30004	4879	244758
	Total	194131	77429	36919	6259	314738
2007	Female	29296	5533	8267	1056	44152
	Male	69789	34891	26121	1949	132750
	Total	99085	40424	34388	3005	176902

I want to be able to see the graph like this:

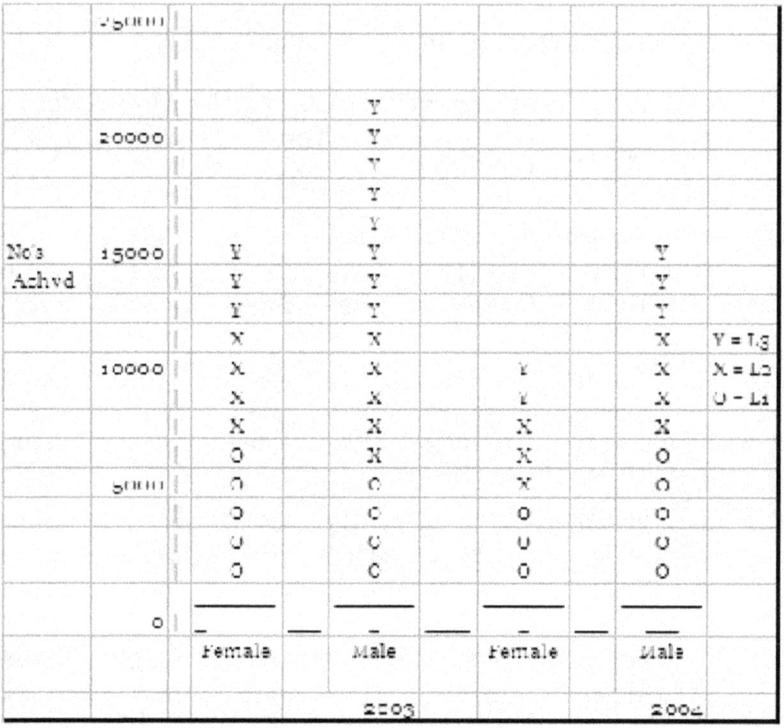

	25000							
				Y				
	20000			Y				
				Y				
				Y				
				Y				
No's	15000	Y		Y			Y	
Achvd		Y		Y			Y	
		Y		Y			Y	
		X		X			X	Y = L3
	10000	X		X	Y		X	X = L2
		X		X	Y		X	O - L1
		X		X	X		X	
		O		X	X		O	
	5000	O		O	X		O	
		O		O	O		O	
		O		O	O		O	
		O		O	O		O	
	0							
		Female		Male	Female		Male	
				2003			2004	

When I use the Charting Expert in CRXI (R2) and set up the advanced screen for "on change of" Date and on change of "Gender", I can only have one value in the Show Value(s) box.

If I select more than one value to show and then select OK, I get a dialog box saying I can have one "on change of" and many values OR many "on change of but only ONE value.

Excel does what I want from a Crystal exported table in selecting the data area, click on the Chart Expert, select the stacked bar and click on OK. Job done.

Is there any solution to this?

A: Try this formula; call it YR-GEN:

totext({Year},0) &" "& totext({Gender})

Then your "on change of" would be @YR-GEN, your show values can be all your levels. Now except for getting the graph to show those X, Y, etc.... you should be much closer.

Question 24: Suppressing fields with null values

I'm trying to find out how to suppress a field in a graph that has a null value. The reason for this is that there is not enough room on the graph to display all fields and it would clean the graph up a great deal.

Is there a way to do this?

A: Suppressing a null value in a graph or not may not be possible. But for your reason doing that, you can try the following solution:

Create a new formula field to replace the existing group(X) axis field: if the field has a null value then specify an empty value, otherwise take the original value. You can create another formula field to reorder the group(X) axis such that the empty value is the last value and all other value in the group(X) axis keeps same order. In this case, all null values take only on position (the last one in right-hand-side) and show nothing.

Question 25: Customizing data series

I have a graph lines report with several (8) data series. On the design chart, there are only 4 lines displayed. I want to change the representation of these data series so that the first 6 are with dot only and the 2 last with lines only. The problem is that I can access only to the 4 first "lines".

How can I modify the other 4 data series?

A: Try to go to the preview page > click the chart> click the series you want to format > right click > select "series options".

Question 26: Chart w/ multiple scales

I'm using CR XI Release 2. Is it possible to create a chart with multiple scales or plot multiple measures on a single chart?

A: Yes. In the Chart selection tab, start out with a "Dual-Y" chart. This will produce a bar/line/area chart that has a y1 scale on the left and y2 scale on the right. Each measure can be mapped to either Y1 or Y2.

Question 27: Unable to use "Series Options"

I have four data series (line graphs). I want to convert one of them to bar graph. I am unable to see "Series Options" after right clicking line graphs. The right clicked menu items are Format Object, Chart Expert, Chart Options, Cut, Copy, Paste, and Delete. There is no "Series Options".

How to get "Series Option" in the right-clicked menu of CR 10/11?

A: You need to be in the graph. Once you are on the graph, select the line you wish to convert. Then right click on the line. That should give you what you need.

Question 28: Dynamic chart height

I have created a horizontal bar chart with the amount of horizontal bars being decided at run-time.

Is there any version of crystal reports to dynamically increase the height of the chart in order to accommodate the amount of bars on my graph while keeping the bar thicknesses constant?

A: You can create a sub report that mimics the legend and is in fact a lot more flexible. Have the legend sub report and chart overlaying each other in order to get them side by side. You can also get the right colors to appear in the legend using mod 17 on the group count and a big select statement. This is possible because crystal charts uses 17 colors in a predictable order.

Having the legend as a sub report can give you a lot of flexibility on its formatting.

Question 29: Reduce number of labels on a line type chart

I have line type chart: data (Y axis) vs. date-time (X axis). Since there are too many date-time metrics and labels, I tried to use in ignore labels and put a number 8 for example, to group some date-time but and messages tell me that you can only use 1 or 2. How can I reduce the number of labels on a line type chart?

A: Try the following steps:

1) Right click on the chart and select "Auto Arrange" option.

2) Click on an x-axis label and bring up the grid/scales dialog. Go to the "Skip" menu and enter a big value so it will skip most x-axis labels.

Question 30: Show all days of month

I run a monthly report and in this report there is a simple bar graph that counts the number of entries of a field for each day of the month. I do this by setting the "On Change of" in the graph expert to a formula named 'Date Only' which is simply Date ({time field linked to entries I am counting}). The problem with this is that if there are no entries to count on a certain date, the bar graph skips that date and displays the next date that has data. This is what you would expect because of the formula I am using. How could I display every date in the month on the bar graph even if there are no entries for some days?

A: Crystal doesn't know that it's a "day of the month" you're reporting on and so it doesn't fill in the sequence. You can work around this by cheating.

Create a table in the source system that had one field in it called DayOfTheMonth and insert 31 records in it... 1, 2, 3, 4, 5, etc. Make this the first file in your data selection and put an outer join not enforced between that and your actual data file linking on the day number. Then summarized on the day number in your cheat file and the outer join will make sure that you have thirty one records in your report, some with data and some without.

Question 31: Converting a bar chart to a line graph

I'm using Crystal Reports XI and I'm trying to convert a bar chart into a line graph. The bar chart has 3 sets of values which I want to split out as three separate points.

A simple conversion to line graph will place the points on a vertical line as the "change of" is the same for the three values. This is obviously I don't want to do.

I want to create a small table from the table I am working on. I believe I need to create a variable for the "on change of" value and then to access an array to place the data on the line graph. Is there a way to do this?

A: You need to do a "swap" of data to make your series into groups and your groups into series. This is a right-mouse menu option in XI.

Question 32: Create a mixed bar/line chart

Our development environment is BO Enterprise IX.

I have to develop a report to show with one chart which will have a bar chart and line chart on top of that with 2 y-axis. When I say line chart, I am not talking about "Trend Lines" of the Crystal Report.

Is it possible to do a mixed chart types?

A: Create two series for your two series of bars in a bar chart.

Then highlight one of the series of bars and go to series and change it from Riser to Line

Question 33: Creating a frequency distribution

I have data in the form of:

Channel (int)
Duration (minutes)

How can I get crystal to create a frequency distribution in the form of:

Channel
0-5 minutes
6-10 minutes
11-

I need to be able to answer for each channel what is the distribution of viewing times in minutes using those classes described above. The closest I can get is a bar chart but this doesn't provide percentages and is not suitable.

How can I achieve this?

A: Set up a formula like:

IF {table.duration} < 6 then 'A 0-5 Minutes'
else if {table.duration} in [6 to 10] then 'B 6-10 Minutes'
else . . .

Group first on channel, then on this formula.

You can create a second formula to strip off the lead characters and use that as your label.

From there it should be easy to graph as a pie chart or stacked bar.

Question 34: Keeping series color

I need to make a series of reports with charts. On each chart I want to set the color to be a specific choice. ChoiceA is red, ChoiceB is blue, etc.

I've gone in to the Chart Expert, Options, Chart color, Format and set each choice to a specific color.

How can I copy these choices or set this as a template so any new report will use the same series color choices and I don't have to go in and set each series value to its specific color?

A: You should have an option to format the color if you deselect the automatically set chart options check box in the chart expert and then go to options.

Question 35: Color of data in legend

I grouped by regions and each region shows units of products sold in last 3 years. There are 5 different products. I inserted a pie chart in GH#1 (Region). It works fine except legend.

Product#1 for Region#1 is indicated in Yellow but the same Product#1 is indicated in Red in Region#2. Problems seem to happen when Regions did not sell all 5 products.

How can I make the color for one product consistent throughout the all regions in CR 10?

A: Try to conditionally format the chart, so that Product #1 is always Yellow, Product #2 is always Red, etc.

You can find this information in the "Help" menu in Crystal 10:

Conditionally formatting a chart:
On the Design or Preview tab, right-click the chart to bring up the shortcut menu.

On the shortcut menu, click Chart Expert.

Clear "Automatically set chart options" if it is selected, and click the Options tab.
In the Chart color area, select Color.

To set conditional color formatting, click the Format button and use the Chart Color Format Expert to set your conditions.

Question 36: Data axis range

In a simple report, I have a Bar chart. When all the values are equal to 0. The range of the chart is from -6 to 6. The chart is in 3D, so when the values are 0, I see a little flat square at the middle of my chart. I don't want that. I want the range of the data axis to be from 0 to the highest value that I have.

Is there a way to set the range so that the minimum is always 0, while the maximum isn't a fixed value?

A: Click on chart. Right mouse menu ChartOptions->Grid.

Then select "Data axis". Then select SCALE tab and put in manual values that you want.

Question 37: Split bar graph into multiple pages

I have a bar graph and it is too long, how can I to split it into multiple pages?

A: The only way to do that is to insert multiple sub reports. Each report should contain a bar graph with a portion of your x-axis values and each report has each section contain a sub report set to New Page Before.

Question 38: Graph Y-axis values

I need to show a graph in a report but I don't know the range of possible values except that they are positive numbers without decimal fraction (figures are numbers of user sessions).

I want to let Crystal determine the range of the y-axis but I don't know if it will be only a few or by the hundreds.

When I select chart expert and set the minor step of the graph to 1 then the output of the graphs behaves differently.

If there are days with lots of user sessions then there are no y values with fractions. If, for the whole period, the maximum y value is 2, then Crystal selects a max range of 2 but his minor step will be like 0.4 and you will have marks for 1.2, 1.6 and so on. How can I do this correctly?

A: You can't set the Y-axis values on a dynamic basis but you can create multiple charts in different sections then conditionally suppress those charts that don't fit the criteria via parameter values entered by the user.

Question 39: Plot zeros on graph for no data

Is it possible to use a data value (0) when data is missing? I am summarizing data using a count of data for each day. Some days have no records.

E.g. I have 5 days of interest but only have data on day 1, 2 and 5. The count works for all of the days with data. The days without data have no results. Problem is that when plotted on a graph it is plotted as if day 1, 2, and 5 are consecutive days. I want to plot the intervening dates showing the graph dip to zero on those days.

A: If the graph won't let you plot zeroes for data that does not exist, you must give it some data to plot.

You could implement this by using a different SQL statement. It should generate a record for each day or month. This was done before by using a "Generate records" table/query that can be left-joined to the record you already have.

Question 40: Plot column and line graph in a single chart

Is there a way to create a chart where I can display a line graph for one series and a bar for another series?

I am trying to add a moving average but the built-in trendline does not accomplish what I need. I tried moving avg series to the graph and added a "connected line" trendline and then tried to turn the bars invisible but it turned the line invisible as well.

A: Create you graph as a bar graph. Then right click on the bar you want to make a line and select chart options then Series. Click the General tab and select 'Line' in the Always show selected series as drop down.

Question 41: Clickable chart

I want to be able to click on a bar on the chart and see the data for that bar.

Is it possible to make a chart interactive?

A: Group your report on the same field you're using in the chart for "On Change Of".

Make sure you create subtotals in the group footers (summaries) on the same field you're using in the chart for "Show Value(s)".

Ensure that you create a GROUP chart rather than an advanced chart. You cannot drill down from an advanced chart but only from a Group chart.

CRYSTAL REPORT: Exporting

Question 42: Stop merging cells

How do I stop crystal from merging cells when exporting to Excel?

The only way I have found to get it not merge cells is when exporting straight out of Crystal reports XI is to set the column width to 288. However this option is not available when using Report Distribution Manager.

A: Use gridlines in design mode, and lock your fields to the gridlines. Be sure that fields in sections above and below your details are also locked to the gridlines. The fields don't necessarily have to be the same width but shouldn't end mid-field on fields above or below. Sometimes adding an empty text field can help in lining up the columns. It can be a bit of a pain depending on the complexity of your report, but you can get past having merged cells via this method.

Question 43: Export to ODBC error

I'm using CR XI and trying to export a Crystal report to an Access database. I have set up the data sources, but when I try to export, I get the error: "Failed to export the report. There is no valid data source for this report. ODBC export cancelled". Then I tried to export to other ODBC formats to test but the result is the same. How can I rectify this error?

A: Exporting requires that the output of the report be in a table format. In addition, an export means that you are creating and writing to a new table, Crystal won't append or insert data into an existing table.

Question 44: Show gridlines as a default

How do I show gridlines as a default when exporting to excel?

The problem for me is that Java is making the call to the Crystal server and by default show gridlines is not set.

Can I set it to 'On' by default?

A: This is a known problem in Excel export. Ensure that excel compatibility patch is applied for your crystal server. Also, if you are using Crystal APIs using Java then use the showGridLine() function.

Question 45: Supporting rpt navigation in Adobe

I am using XI R2, both Crystal and BOE. I have a report which is quite massive.

The only way it can be successfully utilized is to drive it by the group tree on the left. The trouble is, when I export this to PDF, Adobe replaces the group tree with its own page preview navigation thing, which is useless.

Is there a way to supersede this in Adobe and force it to replicate the crystal viewer group tree?

Or, is it possible to create the same thing in an html file that can be attached to an email and viewed offline but keeping the group tree navigation?

A: CRXIR2 allows you to save export options along with your report.

1. Open your report and go to File > Export > Report Export Options.
2. Select Adobe Acrobat (PDF) and click "OK".
3. Check "Create bookmarks from group tree" and click "OK".
4. Re-save your report to Crystal Enterprise.

Now, whenever a user exports *this* report from InfoView *to PDF*, the PDF will have a bookmark section created.

You need to set the Export Options for every report individually. As far as I know, there is no way to do this globally (e.g. say that all PDF exports will always contain a group tree).

It seems that in XI, Business Objects took away the ability for InfoView users to control how their reports export and now expect designers to specifically set how each report can be exported in each format.

Question 46: Crystal Reports viewer will not export

When viewing a report within InfoView using the Crystal Reports Viewer, it will not allow me to export the report to any other format. When I click on the "Export this Report" button, the report just kind of flasheds and there is no dialog box to choose a format to exit to. I am using the DHTML viewer. I am logging on as Administrator. When I have a colleague log in, on her computer, also as Administrator, she does get the dialog box for format to export to.

What steps should I take to correct his?

A: Check your browser settings and be sure pop-ups are not blocked. Also check any toolbars you have added (like Google's) as they have pop-up blockers as well.

Question 47: Exporting Crystal with sub report to Excel

I am currently on Crystal 11 professional and have a report in which one the columns is a sub report. The sub report is in the last column of the main report. The report looks good but whenever I export this to excel, whether it's typical or custom export, my sub report prints on the bottom of the first column (basically it wraps).

How can I format the report so it doesn't wrap?

A: Align the sub report with gridlines, both left and right and bottom (as you should with all columns for exporting). Select all the fields in the same row along with the sub report->format->make same size->height as this ensures the sub report didn't wrap.

Question 48: Export "raw" data from multi grouped report

Is there a way to export a raw flat file version of the data in a highly formatted and several grouped report in Crystal XI R2?

A: This means a fixed field files without a header. One trick is to present a parameter which asks whether this is for export to a text file. If they select yes, suppress every section on your current report and unsuppressed a detail section that just has the fields in it in the format you want and the users can then export to text.

Question 49: Export to PDF changes font on server

We have CRXISR2 reports in our ASP.NET 2.0 application running on an IIS6 Win2K3 server.

The predominant font our reports are written in is Arial Narrow. When the reports render in the CR viewer (i.e. on the Web page), the fonts are showing correctly. On the development machine, the Arial Narrow is rendered properly rendered on the PDF export, but on the server, the font is changed to Arial causing the layout to break on many reports.

Is there a way to fix this?

A: Try using Release 1 instead of Release 2 DLLs. Sometimes R2 DLLs with get buggy once installed on a server.

We have the same problem (although not about fonts) where I have R2 on my development machine and everything works fine but on the server with R2 the reports go crazy. After we reverted back to R1 on our server, it was fixed.

Question 50: Export to text is wrapping

I have a crystal XI report that we export to text and send to our bank to prevent check fraud. The output consists of a series of strings each of which are 242 characters long.

The only problem is the text is wrapping when we open it in notepad. Text Wrap is turned off in notepad. How can we fix this?

A: We use CR XI and my report has a string of 400 characters. Since I have to use a page size of 8.5x11 inches, we had to change my font to Courier New with a size of 2.

When we export it to text and open it with notepad, I had to change the font in Notepad also to Courier New 2. It works perfectly.

Question 51: Export Excel blank space

I am using CR XI and an SQL database. I have a report and my data is fine but when I select export to Microsoft Excel 97-2000-data only, my data has some blank rows between some of my records.

Example:
1 3 5
2 5 3
4
5
6 8 9
7 1 3
8
9 4 5

What is causing this?

A: Try selecting the entire row fields->format->make same size->height. It also helps to have the fields snapped to horizontal and vertical gridlines.

CRYSTAL REPORT:Data connectivity and Access

Question 52: New fields added to stored procedure not visible

I have a Crystal 10 Report that is executing an MS SQL 2000 stored procedure. I modified the stored procedure by adding an additional column. The column was appended as the field in the select clause of the returning SQL statement. This new field is not showing up in my report. I have tried log off/log on and refresh.

I have tried closing crystal application and re-opening. How can I get the new sp field to show up in crystal fields?

A: Use Database->Verify Database.

Question 53: SQL command in a sub report

I have a sub report in the detail section of my main report. The sub report uses an SQL command to get data. I need to pass a field value from the main report to the sub report to use as a parameter in the SQL command in the sub report.

Main report has the field EMPLOYEE.EMPLOYEEID. In the sub report, SQL command, I have - Select min(shiftstartdtm), max(shiftenddtm) from sched where empid={?Pm-EMPLOYEE.EMPLOYEEID} group by calendar date.

When I try to do that, I get an error "failed to retrieve data from the database. Details: HY000:{Oracle][ODBC][Ora]ORA-24374: define not done before fetch or execute and fetch [Database Vendor Code: 24374].

I am using crystal reports XI and Oracle database.

What is causing this error?

A: Try changing the command to:

Select min(shiftstartdtm),max(shiftenddtm), empid
from sched
group by empid, calendar date

Then in the main report, link the sub report to the main report by linking {EMPLOYEE.EMPLOYEEID} to {command.empid}.

Question 54: Database connector error

I am using Crystal 11 and publish through the console manager. I have a report that displays fine in Crystal, but when I publish it I get an error "Database Connector Error". I don't use any passwords or user names on my reports. This report access a query that the other reports do not use. I can run the query in the database just fine. I also restored a backup of this query but that did not solve the problem either.

I tried deleting the report out of the console and re-saved it but I am still getting the same error. What is the cause of this error? How can I fix it?

A: The error is being caused by you reporting off an Access database. This happens because the Crystal/Business Objects Enterprise services start using the Local system account. You need to change these services to use a domain account that has access permissions to your access database.

The services you need to use the domain account with are:

Crystal Reports Job Server: For scheduled report jobs

Crystal Page Server: For view on demand reports using DHTML, ActiveX and Java viewers

Report Application Server: For view on demand reports using the Advanced DHTML viewer.

Question 55: Default value as a formula

I am using stored procedures from both SQL Server 2000 and 2005 with Crystal XI.

I need to schedule a report which has a date parameter and have it run daily. Can the default value for the parameter be "Today"? The only way of setting the default value for a date parameter is to select an actual date and not a formula.

Is it possible to do this?

A: Go into the parameter in Crystal and set the default date to 1/1/1970.

Then code the SP to default to getdate() when passed 1/1/1970, otherwise use what is passed.

Question 56: Connect error when running in BOE

I'm using Crystal XI and Oracle 8i database using an Oracle ODBC driver.

I am using the add command to link two table from two separate databases, SID76 and SID70. The remote Database link was created separately and is the following:

```
CODE:
create public database link sid70.world
connect to prduser identified by abc123
using 'SID70';
```

I have the following add command that runs fine in Crystal XI developer. From the report I am logged into SID76 database.

```
CODE:
SELECT
   '7.6' "DB",
    MASTER_NAMES."LNAME",
   MASTER_NAMES."FNAME",
   MASTER_NAMES."MNAME",
   MASTER_NAMES."MN_ID",
   MASTER_NAMES."PER_PERSON_ID"
FROM
   "PRDDBA"."MASTER_NAMES" MASTER_NAMES
WHERE
   MASTER_NAMES."LNAME" = UPPER( '{?LName}') AND
   MASTER_NAMES."FNAME" = UPPER('{?FName}')
UNION
SELECT
   '7.0' "DB",
    MASTER_NAMES70."LNAME",
   MASTER_NAMES70."FNAME",
   MASTER_NAMES70."MNAME",
   MASTER_NAMES70."MN_ID",
   MASTER_NAMES70."PER_PERSON_ID"
FROM
   "PRDDBA"."MASTER_NAMES"@SID70.WORLD MASTER_NAMES70
WHERE
   MASTER_NAMES70."LNAME" = UPPER('{?LName}') AND
   MASTER_NAMES70."FNAME" = UPPER('{?FName}');
```

The report runs fine in Crystal XI but I get the following error when I try to run the same report in BO Enterprise using either the CMC preview mode or Infoview:

> "Failed to open the connection. Master_Name Command.rpt
> Unable to retrieve Object.
> Failed to open the connection. Master_Name Command.rpt"

It appears that it does not recognize the remote connection. What steps should I take to correct this error?

A: Make sure that the CE server has an Oracle client on it or CE can't access the database at all. Try creating a view in SID76 that uses that same code. Base your report on the view then publish and see if it works.

Try installing Crystal Reports on the CE server so that you can test these types of things as it tends to provide better error messages.

Question 57: Max records limit reached

I get the following error when I preview a crystal report (Crystal XI) on Business Objects. There are approximately 30 million records in the Oracle database for this report:

"Error in File All Sensor Readings between 2 dates and times (Summary).rpt: Max processing time or Max records limit reached".

How do I work around this?

A: This error message appears because the Crystal Reports Page Server and Report Application Server (RAS) return a maximum of 20,000 records by default.

To resolve this error message for the Page Server:

1. Go to Start > Programs > BusinessObjects XI > BusinessObjects Enterprise (or Crystal Reports Server) > Central Management Console.
2. Log into the CMC with an Administrator's account.
3. Click 'Servers', and then click the 'Crystal Reports Page Server'.
4. Under the 'Properties' tab, change the option 'Database Records to Read When Previewing or Refreshing a Report' to 'Unlimited'.
5. Click 'Update'.
6. Restart the Crystal Reports Page Server service.

To resolve this error message for the RAS Server:

1. Go to Start > Programs > BusinessObjects XI > BusinessObjects Enterprise (or Crystal Reports Server) > Central Configuration Manager.
2. Click 'Report Application Server' and then click the 'Stop' button.
3. Right-click 'Report Application Server', and then click 'Properties'. The 'Report Application Server Properties' dialog box appears.

4. On the 'Parameters' tab, in the 'Option Type' list, click 'Database'.
5. Under 'Max Number of Records', click 'Unlimited', and then click 'OK'.
6. Restart the 'Crystal Report Application Server' service.

After completing the above steps, you should be able to successfully preview the report.

Use the following notes to determine which server needs to have its limits increased when viewing reports in InfoView:

- If the report is previewed in the DHTML, ActiveX, or Java viewers in InfoView, report is being processed by the Page Server.

- If the report is previewed in the Advanced DHTML viewer in InfoView, the report is being processed by the Report Application Server.

Use the following notes to determine which server needs to have its limits increased when viewing reports from a custom BusinessObjects Enterprise or Crystal Reports Server .NET, COM, or Java SDK based application:

- For custom applications, if the report source that is passed to the viewer is obtained from the 'PSReportFactory', the report will be processed by the Page Server, unless it is passed to the CrystalReportInteractiveViewer (in which case RAS will process the report).

- For custom applications, if the report source that is passed to the viewer is obtained from the 'RptAppFactory', the report will be processed by RAS.

Question 58: Table Joins

I am linking two tables using Crystal X. Table A is a Bill of Material Table and it has multiple records for a distinct item. Table B is a Qty on hand table and it also has multiple records for a distinct item number.

Example:

Table A

PPN	ITEM NUMBER
Widget	Gadget
Test	Gadget

Table B

ITEM NUMBER	LOCATION	QTY
Gadget	NORTH	20
Gadget	WAREHOUSE	10

The two tables are linked by Item Number from Table A to Table B.

Current Results (in detail section of report)

Gadget NORTH 20
Gadget NORTH 20
Gadget WAREHOUSE 10
Gadget WAREHOUSE 10

Desired Results:
Gadget NORTH 20
Gadget WAREHOUSE 10

Since there are two records in Table A for Gadget, the report duplicates and prints two records for every individual record in Table B. If only one record for item number is in Table A, the report prints fine. If there are three records in Table A then 3 records for every individual record prints.

How can I achieve the desired results?

A: You could try going to database->select distinct records. Also try concatenating the three fields and then insert a group on the formula:

```
{tableB.ITEM
NUMBER}+{tableB.LOCATION}+totext({tableB.QTY},0,"")
```

Then place the detail fields in the group header or footer instead of the groupname.

Question 59: Two unique tables/single report

I use CR XI and my data sources are Foxpro tables accessed via ODBC.

There are two unique tables which do not link. One is the AP check file and the other is the cash receipts file. I need to do a report wherein I can calculate the total of the checks issued for a period of time and the total of the cash received for the same period. Then I need to do another calculation based on the result of the two formulas.

Is there a way to do this?

A: Try to create a command as the data source with a UNION ALL select statement. By including a column to indicate the type of record ("check" or "cash"), you can easily create conditional totals to sum each separately.

```
SELECT check_date, check_amount, "check" as TYPE from CHECKS
UNION ALL
SELECT cash_date, cash_amount, "cash" from CASH_RECEIPTS
```

This may not only perform slightly faster but also form the basis for other reporting needs.

Question 60: Access a different datasource

I'm using CR 11 with MS ODBC for Visual Fox Pro.

I have 3 different databases against which I need the same format. For example, one report runs against a table called arcust02 from data source data02. The format of the elements in the table are arcust02.custno; arcust02.company, etc.

I need to run the same report against arcust01 from data source data01 which has the same layout as arcust02. I do not want to rewrite any reports which fall into this category.

How can I change the reports to access a different data source without rewriting the reports?

A: Save the report under another name and use Database->Set Location and point to the other database.

Question 61: Get related data but not joined data

I'm using a Crystal XI with Access 2003.

I have two separate tables; one that contains data about employee authorizations (AUTHORIZATIONS) and the other that contains data about employee enrolled (ENROLLED) in courses. These tables don't share a unique identifier.

From the AUTHORIZATIONS table I need to capture the "department", "job specialty" and a count of "position number" (primary key). This will produce the number of positions for a "job specialty" within each "department".

From the ENROLLED table I need the "department", "job specialty" and count of "enrolled number" (primary key). This will produce the number of enrolled for a "job specialty" within each "department".

I've been able to do this without any problem. The problem comes when I want to show the data side-by-side. For example:

Department:

Job Specialty (Count of Pos#) (Count of Enrollment#)

I've been able to be successful in displaying the values in which the "job specialty" exists in the "department" in both tables, but when the "job specialty" only exists in one of the tables, I don't get a result.

For example: The AUTHORIZATIONS table contains records for "job specialty" (xyz), but there aren't any records in the ENROLLED table for "job specialty" (xyz) and vice versa.

How do I get the report to show all instances of "job specialty" from both tables and then provide the value?

A: One such method might be to create a UNION ALL in either an Access query to return all data, or you can use an Add Command listed under the Access data connection to paste in the SQL to do this.

Something like:

```
select 'auth' tbl, department, specialty, number from auth
UNION ALL
select 'enr' tbl, department, specialty, number from enr
```

Then you can group by the department and specialty and provide conditional counts using Running Totals and in the evaluate->use a formula place the criteria for each, as in:

tbl = "AUTH"

Question 62: Show consecutive date ranges

I have a Crystal Report that pulls a record for each day an employee works. I am grouping all the employee records and further grouping the employees by Supervisor.

I am trying to show on the group2 Footer the maximum consecutive days the employee did not work in the period.

I can show the various breaks by subtracting the previous work date from the work date at the detail level but cannot show in the group 2 footer the maximum # of days break in the period.

For example:

```
              Day Worked
Employee one   9/1/2006
Employee one   9/2/2006
Employee one   9/4/2006
Employee one   9/8/2006
Employee one   9/9/2006
Employee one   9/10/2006

Group 2 footer
Employee one   Days worked  Max # of consecutive off
           6   3
```

How can I show in the group 2 footer the maximum # of days break in the period?

A: Use a variable to collect the maximum. Let's say your difference formula is {@gap}:

if previous({table.emplID}) = {table.emplID} then
datediff("d", previous({table.date}), {table.date})

Then use a formula like the following in the detail section:

whileprintingrecords;

```
numbervar maxgap;
if {@gap} > maxgap then
maxgap := {@gap};
```

In the group footer for employee, use:

```
whileprintingrecords;
numbervar maxgap;
```

In the group header for employee, use:

```
whileprintingrecords;
numbervar maxgap := 0;
```

Question 63: Updating data source location

I have a report that has a simple sub report. In the sub report it just lists 3 columns and stores them in an array for use by the main report.

I need to add a little more logic to this sub report and created a command that has the correct query. However, when I try to change the data source from the table to the command nothing happens.

What am I doing wrong?

A: Create the Command on a separate report. Once it is created, save it to the Repository from the Database Expert. After you have saved it, you can go back to the original report and do the 'Set Location'.

To find the Command, the last category in the Database Expert is "Repository"

Question 64: "Keep together" not working

I am using CR XI sp2 running on WIN XP. I have a group header with the "Keep together" option checked in the section expert. However, the header will print on a page without room for the rest of the group. I have other groups that are working correctly, that are set up the same way.

Is my procedure correct?

A: "Keep together" on a section only refers to keeping together that report section, not the group. To keep together an entire group, go to report->group expert->select the group->options tab->check "keep group together".

Question 65: Crystal reports slowness

I'm using Crystal Reports XI and SQL Server 2003. I'm trying to develop a crystal report which connects to a stored procedure through an ODBC connection. When trying to insert a field or label into the report it's extremely slow. I've check the server and the server is fine as well as the ODBC connection. What might be causing this?

A: Problems occur with Crystal Reports 10 and 11 if a strange printer was selected as the default printer, selecting a real printer or even a 'pretend' laser printer.

It looked like something was causing problems with the screen redisplay.

Select a different default printer or set the report printer settings to "NO Printer".

Question 66: Make a sum

I have a table with 3 fields in my database:

table(id,amount,theboolean)

A report displaying the "amount" field for each row in the table is made. I need to display "amount" only if "theboolean" is true and when "theboolean" is false and display the "sum(amount) where theboolean=false" at the end of the report.

How can I do this in Crystal Reports XI?

A: You need to eliminate the false records from your report with a record selection formula. Go to report, selection formulas, record and enter a simple formula:

{theBoolean}

Get this formula by double clicking on the field name. Normally, a record selection formula must evaluate to true or false (ex: {CustName} Startswith "A") but in your case your field is a boolean, so you just need to place the field itself in the record selection formula.

To get your sum, go to the report canvas and right click the field you want summed and select insert, grand total.

Or remove the record selection formula and instead put it in the Group selection area (report->selection formula->GROUP). Now you will have only the records with True displayed but the other records are available in the report. Create a formula and place it in the detail section:

if {table.theboolean} = false then {table.amount}

Right click on this and insert a grand total (sum). You can do the same for the true records.

Question 67: Rename column headings in crosstab

I'm using CRXI. I have a crosstab that has a date field in the row. In the column it is based on a code that has been typed in the database. Is it possible to rename the column headings to read a name associated with the code that has been typed in?

I have had some success and can get it to rename based on one of the codes using the "display string" under common under format field. This is what I have so far but all the columns come back "OUT OF COUNTY".

```
If {sys_trac.actioncode} = "ICX" THEN "IN COUNTY"
  ELSE "OUT OF COUNTY"

// NEED TO CONVERT THE FOLLOWING CODES TO FULL
NAMES
// ICX TO "IN COUNTY"
// OCX TO "OUT OF COUNTY"
// SS TO "SALES"
```

A: In the crosstab expert, select the column->group options->options tab->customize group name->use formula as group name->x+2 and enter the following formula there:

```
select {sys_trac.actioncode}
case "ICX" : "IN COUNTY"
case "OCX" : "OUT OF COUNTY"
case "SS" : "SALES"
```

Question 68: Select report's data source at runtime

I want to use CRXI to link to 1 of many identically structured CSV files via ODBC. Each one is a list of invoice details.

I want to pass a parameter to CRXI indicating the name of the datasource (a CSV file) to be read for a particular instance of the report. I have considered that I can rename the desired file to a fixed name that that the report will always reference. However, I would prefer to be able to pass a parameter instead. Is this possible?

A: Yes. Create an ODBC connection (text driver) to the CSV file.

Now in the Database Expert, select ODBC and point to the 'Add Command' instead of pointing at the file directly.

In the SQL use:

select * from c:\

Create a parameter of type string and then double click it and it will insert it into the SQL statement.

Question 69: Date field / Parameters / Nulls

I'm trying to use parameters to filter data on a date field (basically between a start and end date). That part works fine but I also need it to pull out NULL values as well which it's not doing. Here's what I have:

```
CODE:
... and

(({s_BondTracking;1.ReleaseDate}                        >=
{?ReleaseDateBegin}
                                          and
```

```
{s_BondTracking;1.ReleaseDate} <= {?ReleaseDateEnd})
OR
IsNull({s_BondTracking;1.ReleaseDate})
OR
{s_BondTracking;1.ReleaseDate} = Date(0,0,0))
```

and ...

Now when I run this, I get ReleaseDates between the before & end dates (good) but I'm not getting records that also have NULL release dates (bad). What am I doing wrong?

A: Always check for nulls first. Change the formula to:

```
and
(
IsNull({s_BondTracking;1.ReleaseDate}) or
{s_BondTracking;1.ReleaseDate} = Date(0,0,0)or
(
{s_BondTracking;1.ReleaseDate} >= {?ReleaseDateBegin} and
{s_BondTracking;1.ReleaseDate} <= {?ReleaseDateEnd}
)
```

Question 70: Make running total fields print 0 values

I am using CR XI full version and a dbase database.

I have created a running total field that computes a weighted average value that resets on a change of group.

When the weighted average value is zero, it will print nothing. I would like it to print 0 instead of nothing. I have looked to see if this is a report option but could not find anything. How can I do that?

A: Right click on the running total->format field->number->customize and see if "suppress if zero" is checked. If not, you might have a null somewhere that is causing a null running total. You could either go to file->report options->and check "convert nulls to default value" or, you could write a formula like:

if isnull({#yourrunningtotal}) then 0 else
{#yourrunningtotal}

Question 71: Show nulls only in report

I have a report that shows username, department number and IDnumber. I would like to show only users that have no value or null in the IDnumber field. How can I do this?

A: One way is to create a record selection formula of:

IsNull({IDnumber}) or Trim({IDnumber}) = ""

CRYSTAL REPORT: Formula

Question 72: Display parameters chosen using a formula

I'm using Crystal Reports XI and have a report that has 7 parameters which a user can select any or all. I would like to show the user's selection criteria on the report or page header. I wrote the following into a formula that was in that report header.

If {?Gender} <> "All" Then "Gender; " & {?Gender} and

If {?Sponsor} <> "All" Then "Sponsor: " & {?Sponsor}

But got this error:

"A boolean is required here" with the "Gender; " & {?Gender} section highlighted. It works fine with only a single IF statement but has problems when you add multiple IF statements. What is wrong with my formula?

A: Your syntax is off. As an example:

Displaying the parameter choices made for the user:

```
STRING PARAMETERS:

Discrete:

{?MyStringParameter}

Range value separated by " to ":

Minimum({?MyStringParameter})&"          to          "&
Maximum({?MyStringParameter})

Multiple Discrete values separated by a comma:

join({?MyStringParameter},",")

Multiple Range values separated by a carriage return:

whileprintingrecords;
```

```
stringvar Output:="";
numbervar Counter;
For Counter := 1 to ubound({?MyStringParameter}) do(
Output:=
Output&minimum({?MyStringParameter}[Counter])& " to
"& maximum({?MyStringParameter}[Counter])&chr(13)
);
left(Output,len(Output)-1)
```

Multiple Range and Discrete values separated by a carriage return:

```
whileprintingrecords;
stringvar Output:="";
numbervar Counter;
For Counter := 1 to ubound({?MyStringParameter}) do(
if minimum({?MyStringParameter}[Counter])=
maximum({?MyStringParameter}[Counter]) then
Output:= Output &
minimum({?MyStringParameter}[Counter])&chr(13)
else
Output:= Output &
minimum({?MyStringParameter}[Counter])& " to "&
maximum({?MyStringParameter}[Counter])&chr(13)
);
left(Output,len(Output)-1)
```

NUMERIC PARAMETERS:

Discrete:

```
{?MyNumericParameter}
```

Range value separated by "to":

```
Minimum({?MyNumericParameter})&" to "&
Maximum({?MyNumericParameter})
```

For concerns with decimal precision and thousands separator, use:

```
totext(Minimum({?MyNumericParameter}),0,"")&" to "&
totext(Maximum({?MyNumericParameter}),0,"")
```

Multiple Discrete values separated by a comma:

```
whileprintingrecords;
stringvar Output:="";
numbervar Counter;
```

```
For Counter := 1 to ubound({?MyNumericParameter}) do(
Output:= Output&
totext({?MyNumericParameter}[Counter],0,"")& ","
);
left(Output,len(Output)-1)
```

Multiple Range values separated by a carriage return:

```
whileprintingrecords;
stringvar Output:="";
numbervar Counter;
For Counter := 1 to ubound({?MyNumericParameter}) do(
Output:= Output&
totext(minimum({?MyNumericParameter}[Counter]),0,"")&
" to "&
totext(maximum({?MyNumericParameter}[Counter]),0,"")&
chr(13)
);
left(Output,len(Output)-1)
```

Multiple Range and Discrete values separated by a carriage return:

```
whileprintingrecords;
stringvar Output:="";
numbervar Counter;
For Counter := 1 to ubound({?MyNumericParameter}) do(
if minimum({?MyNumericParameter}[Counter])=
maximum({?MyNumericParameter}[Counter]) then
Output:= Output &
totext(minimum({?MyNumericParameter}[Counter]),0,"")&
chr(13)
else
Output:= Output &
totext(minimum({?MyNumericParameter}[Counter]),0,"")&
" to "&
totext(maximum({?MyNumericParameter}[Counter]),0,"")&
chr(13)
);
left(Output,len(Output)-1)
```

DATE PARAMETERS:

Discrete:

```
{?MyDateParameter}
```

Range value separated by "to":

```
Minimum({?MyDateParameter})&","&
Maximum({?MyDateParameter})
```

Multiple Discrete values separated by a comma:

```
whileprintingrecords;
stringvar Output:="";
numbervar Counter;
For Counter := 1 to ubound({?MyDateParameter}) do(
Output:= Output& {?MyDateParameter}[Counter]& ","
);
left(Output,len(Output)-1)
```

Multiple Range values separated by a carriage return:

```
whileprintingrecords;
stringvar Output:="";
numbervar Counter;
For Counter := 1 to ubound({?MyDateParameter}) do(
Output:=                                          Output&
minimum({?MyDateParameter}[Counter])&    "    to    "&
maximum({?MyDateParameter}[Counter])&chr(13)
);
left(Output,len(Output)-1)
```

Multiple Range and Discrete values separated by a carriage return:

```
whileprintingrecords;
stringvar Output:="";
numbervar Counter;
For Counter := 1 to ubound({?MyDateParameter}) do(
if              minimum({?MyDateParameter}[Counter])=
maximum({?MyDateParameter}[Counter]) then
Output:=                     Output                    &
minimum({?MyDateParameter}[Counter])&chr(13)
else
Output:=                     Output                    &
minimum({?MyDateParameter}[Counter])&    "    to    "&
maximum({?MyDateParameter}[Counter])&chr(13)
);
left(Output,len(Output)-1)
```

As you can see from these examples, the differences between string and numeric (or dates and other data types) is that you must first convert non-string data types to a string, hopefully this will allow you to handle any data types.

Now, if you're bent on doing it all in one formula, then code it accordingly:

```
whileprintingrecords;
stringvar Output:="";
If {?Gender} <> "All" Then
Output:=Output & "Gender; " & {?Gender} & chr(13);
If {?Sponsor} <> "All" Then
Output:=Output & "Sponsor: " & {?Sponsor};
Output
```

Question 73: Basics of totals

What are the ways to find totals in CRX?

A: There are several ways to find totals: running totals, summary totals and variables. Right-click on a field and choose Insert to get a choice of Running Total or Summary. Or else use the Field Explorer, the icon that is a grid-like box, to add running totals.

Running totals allow you to do clever things with grouping and formulas. They also accumulate for each line, hence the name. The disadvantage is that they are working out at the same time as the Crystal report formats the line. You cannot test for their values until after the details have been printed. You can show them in the group footer but not the group header, where they will be zero if you are resetting them for each group.

They also use more machine-time than other types of total, so don't use them without good reason.

Summary totals are based directly on the data. This means that they can be shown in the header. They can also be used to sort groups, or to suppress them. Suppress a group if it has less than three members, say. They default to 'Grand Total', but also can be for a group.

They are more efficient than Running totals, but less flexible.

Variables are user-defined fields. One useful variant are shared variables to pass data from a sub report back to the main report. You can also use variables to show page totals. For normal counting I find running totals or summary totals much easier.

Directly Calculated Totals within a Formula Field can be coded directly, with commands like Sum ({ADV01.Advance}, {ADV01.AccType}). The same result can be achieved by picking up an existing Variable, and will keep the code even if the Variable itself is later deleted. Formula fields can also include Running Totals and other Formula Fields, with some limits depending on when the values are calculated.

It is also possible to get totals using a Formula Field, which can contain a Variable or a Directly Calculated Total.

To get yourself familiar with the idea, try doing a test report with a summary total and a running total for the same field, placed on the detail line. You'll find that the running total increases as each line is printed, whereas the summary total has the final value all along.

For some sorts of totaling, a Crosstab would be a better option. This can group records using values different from the main report. Try Insert > Crosstab and it will guide you through the process.

Question 74: Comparing character in row with next row

I am using CR XI and having trouble with a formula to compare the first 4 characters with the next row first 4 char.

I have a SWCODE field that has 4 or 5 char in it.
0400
0400a
0400b
0401
0402
0402a

My objective is to create a formula to compare the left 4 char to the row below it to see if they match and if so I want to print "Additional Products".

So it would be 0400 Aditional Products
0400a
0400b
0401 Aditional Products

I had thought maybe this might work but I can't tell it to look at the next row of excel:
If Left({Sheet1_.SW Dir Code},4)= (Left({Sheet1_.SW Dir Code},4)+1);

What adjustments should I make?

A: Try:

if left({table.field},4) <> left(previous({table.field},4))

and

left({table.field},4) = next(left({table.field},4)) then "Additional Products"

Question 75: Suppress section when database field is suppressed

I use Crystal XI and Visual basic. One of details section has database field which is never blank. I suppress that field if value is duplicated. How can I suppress whole section if field is suppressed and show if field is not suppressed?

A: Go to the section expert->details->suppress->x+2 and enter:

```
{table.field} = previous({table.field})
```

Question 76: Checking if a value has changed

The value I have in the details section will replicate until the new value is displayed. I want the report to tell when that value has changed. Is there a way in Crystal to check a value in real time?

A: You can do that if it is a field in a section.

The functions are NEXT() and PREVIOUS()

So you can have a formula of:

```
if next(table.field} <> {table.field} then
"It changed"
else
"Same ole..."
```

Question 77: Cross-Tab Question

How can I show a column field in a cross tab that is a sum of two fields?

A: Create a formula that adds the two together, for example:

{table.amt1}+{table.amt2}

Then insert the formula as a summary field.

Question 78: Need report showing stock, sales, purchases

I am using Crystal 10 with a SQL database and need to create a report from the following 4 tables:

Item table contains the ITEMNO, DESC
Stock table contains BIN, ITEMNO, QTY
Sales table contains DOCNO, ITEMNO, ORD_QTY
Purchase table contains PONO, ITEMNO, PURCH_QTY

ITEMNO DESC
Z1 Widgit
Z2 Blue Widgit

BIN ITEMNO Qty
B1 Z1 10
B1 Z2 5
B2 Z2 6
B3 Z2 3

DOCNO ITEMNO Qty
SO100 Z1 5
SO200 Z1 12

PONO ITEMNO Qty
PO100 Z2 100
PO101 Z1 50

Desired Result:
On Hand SO PO
Z1 Widgit 10 17 50
Z2 Blue Widgit 14 0 100

I linked the Item table to the Stock table, Item table to the Sales table and Item table to the Purchase table (via ITEMNO). Since they are 3 independent tables, I can't figure out how to put the fields into the report. What would I group by besides the item number?

A: You can simplify this by using a command to create a union all statement, as in:

```
Select 'Stock' as Type, Item.`ItemNo` as Item, Item.`Desc`,
Stock.`Bin`, Stock.`ItemNo`,Stock.`Qty`
From Item inner join Stock on
Item.`ItemNo` = Stock.`ItemNo`
Union All
Select 'Sales' as Type, Item.`ItemNo` as Item, Item.`Desc`,
Sales.`DocNo`,Sales.`ItemNo`,Sales.`Qty`
From Item inner join Sales on
Item.`ItemNo` = Sales.`ItemNo`
Union All
Select 'Purchase' as Type, Item.`ItemNo` as Item, Item.`Desc`,
Purchase.`PONo`,Purchase.`ItemNo`,Purchase.`Qty`
From Item inner join Purchase on
Item.`ItemNo` = Purchase.`ItemNo`
```

Then you could insert a crosstab that uses {command.ItemNo} as the row field, {command.type} as the column field, and the sum of this formula {@qty} as the summary field:

```
if {command.type} = "Sales" then = -{command.qty} else
{command.qty}
```

Also insert a group on {command.item} and then go to report->selection formula->group and enter:

```
sum({@qty},{command.item}) < 0
```

Question 79: Determine what report uses a particular table

We're using BOXI and have developed reports using Crystal Reports 10 and 11. I have a table name and need to know which reports use that particular table. Is this possible?

A: Here are 2 scripts that will:

1. Retreive all reports in your system (or you can specify a folder if desired) and by clicking on the report id,
2. Call the second page that will show all tables and database information for that report and any subreports it contains.

Main Page:

```
CODE
  <%@ Language=VBScript %>
<% Option Explicit

%>
<HTML>
<HEAD>
<title>BOE XI Reports MetaData Page</title>
<link          rel="stylesheet"          type="text/css"
href="rsc/style/template_style.css"/>
<style type="text/css">
body {
    font-family:Verdana,   Arial,   Helvetica,   sans-
serif;
    font-size:12px;
    color:#5F5F5F;
    text-decoration:none;
    scrollbar-arrow-color:#003366;
    scrollbar-base-color:#C0C0C0;
    scrollbar-darkshadow-color:#6699cc;
    scrollbar-face-color:#6699cc;
    scrollbar-highlight-color:;
    scrollbar-shadow-color:;
}

table {
    font-family:Verdana,   Arial,   Helvetica,   sans-
serif;
```

```
    font-size:12px;
    color:#5F5F5F;
    text-decoration:none;
}

td {
    vertical-align:top;
    }

.dropdown {
    font-size:11px;
    }

.marginTable {
    margin-left: 10px;
    margin-right: 10px;
}

.heading {
    font-size:18px;
    font-weight:700;
    text-align:center;
    color:#003366;
}

.leftnav {
    font-family:arial,helvetica,sans-serif;
    font-weight:bold;
    font-size:12px;
    color:white;
    text-decoration:none;
}

a:hover.leftnav {
    text-decoration:underline;
}

.leftnavHeading {
    font-family:arial,helvetica,sans-serif;
    font-weight:bold;
    font-size:12px;
    text-align:center;
    background-color:#99ccff;
    color:#003366;
    text-decoration:none;
}

a:hover.leftnavHeading {
    text-decoration:underline;
}
```

```
.leftnavHeadingLeftAlign {
    font-family:arial,helvetica,sans-serif;
    font-weight:bold;
    font-size:12px;
    text-align:Left;
    /*background-color:#99ccff;  */
    color:#003366;
    text-decoration:none;
}


.tableHeading {
    font-weight:700;
    color:#003366;
    font-size:14px;
}
.tableHeadingGreen {
    font-weight:700;
    color:green;
    font-size:14px;
}

.tableHeadingLeft {
    font-weight:700;
    text-align:left;
}


.tableHeadingLink {
    font-weight:700;
    color:#5F5F5F;
    text-align:center;
    text-decoration:none;
}

a:hover.tableHeadingLink {
    font-weight:700;
    color:#5F5F5F;
    text-align:center;
    text-decoration:underline;
}

.tableLink {
    font-weight:200;
    font-size:14px;
    color:#003366;
    text-align:left;
```

```
    text-decoration:none;
}

a:hover.tableLink {
    font-weight:200;
    color:#6699cc;
    text-align:left;
    text-decoration:underline;
}

.navigationPage {
    font-size:14px;
    font-weight:700;
    text-align:left;
    color:#003366;
    text-decoration:none;
}

a:hover.navigationPage {
    font-size:14px;
    font-weight:700;
    text-align:left;
    color:#6699cc;
    text-decoration:underline;
}

.emailLink {
    font-weight:200;
    color:#5F5F5F;
    text-align:left;
    text-decoration:underline;
}

a:hover.emailLink {
    font-weight:200;
    color:#333333;
    text-align:left;
    text-decoration:underline;
}
</style>
<Script Language="JavaScript">
    function GetReport(Rid){
         if (Rid > "") {
     location                                           =
"/CeViewer/view_tablesDB.asp?ReportID=" + Rid;
  }
}
</Script>
</HEAD>
```

```
<BODY>

<%

Const APS = "<YOURCMS>"

Const UserID = "<Username>"

Const Password= "<password>"

Const Aut = "secEnterprise"

Function Logon(ByRef IStore)

    Dim SessionManager
    Dim Result
    Result = FALSE
    Set                    SessionManager                    =
Server.CreateObject("CrystalEnterprise.SessionMgr")
    If Err.Number = 0 then
        Dim Sess
        Set    Sess    =    SessionManager.Logon(UserID,
Password, APS, Aut)
        If Err.Number = 0 then
          Set IStore = Sess.Service  ("", "InfoStore")
          Set Session("IStore") = IStore
          Result = TRUE
        End If
    end if
   Logon = Result
End Function

Function MakeWebPage(Reports)
   Dim pRpt
   Dim pRpts
   Dim MyStore
   Response.Write("<HTML>")
   Response.Write("<BODY")
   Response.Write("<FORM Name='main'>")
   Response.Write("<TABLE>")
   Response.Write("<TH
class=tableHeading>Reports</TH>")
   Response.Write("<TR class=tableHeadingGreen>")

Response.Write("<TD>ID</TD><TD>Title</TD><TD>Descript
ion</TD></TR><TR>")
```

```
    Set MyStore = Session("IStore")
    Response.Write("</FORM>")
    Response.Write("<TD>There are " & Reports.Count &
" Reports </TD></TR><TR>")
     for each pRpt in Reports
     Response.Write("<TD>      <A      href='"      &
"JavaScript:GetReport(" & pRpt.ID & ")' >" & pRpt.ID
&  "</a></TD><TD>"  &  pRpt.Title  &  "</TD><TD>"  &
pRpt.Description & "</TD></TR><TR>")
        Next
  Response.Write("</TR></TABLE></BODY></HTML>")
  End Function



Sub Main
   Logon IStore
   Set        Result        =        IStore.Query("Select
SI_ID,SI_NAME,SI_DESCRIPTION    From    CI_INFOOBJECTS
WHERE  SI_PROGID  =  'CrystalEnterprise.Report'  and
SI_INSTANCE = 0 order by SI_NAME" )
   Dim IStore
   Dim Result
   MakeWebPage(Result)

  End Sub

Main
%>
</BODY>
</HTML>



It calls this ( view_tablesDB.asp)
CODE
 <%@ Language=VBScript %>

<% Option Explicit

%>
<HTML>
<HEAD>
<title>BOE XI Reports MetaData Page</title>
<link         rel="stylesheet"         type="text/css"
href="rsc/style/template_style.css"/>
<style type="text/css">
body {
    font-family:Verdana,  Arial,  Helvetica,  sans-
serif;
```

```
    font-size:12px;
    color:#5F5F5F;
    text-decoration:none;
    scrollbar-arrow-color:#003366;
    scrollbar-base-color:#C0C0C0;
    scrollbar-darkshadow-color:#6699cc;
    scrollbar-face-color:#6699cc;
    scrollbar-highlight-color:;
    scrollbar-shadow-color:;
}

table {
    font-family:Verdana,  Arial,  Helvetica,  sans-
serif;
    font-size:12px;
    color:#5F5F5F;
    text-decoration:none;
}

td {
    vertical-align:top;
    }

.dropdown {
    font-size:11px;
    }

.marginTable {
    margin-left: 10px;
    margin-right: 10px;
}

.heading {
    font-size:18px;
    font-weight:700;
    text-align:center;
    color:#003366;
}

.leftnav {
    font-family:arial,helvetica,sans-serif;
    font-weight:bold;
    font-size:12px;
    color:white;
    text-decoration:none;
}

a:hover.leftnav {
```

```
    text-decoration:underline;
}

.leftnavHeading {
    font-family:arial,helvetica,sans-serif;
    font-weight:bold;
    font-size:12px;
    text-align:center;
    background-color:#99ccff;
    color:#003366;
    text-decoration:none;
}

a:hover.leftnavHeading {
    text-decoration:underline;
}

.leftnavHeadingLeftAlign {
    font-family:arial,helvetica,sans-serif;
    font-weight:bold;
    font-size:12px;
    text-align:Left;
    /*background-color:#99ccff;   */
    color:#003366;
    text-decoration:none;
}


.tableHeading {
    font-weight:700;
    color:#003366;
    font-size:14px;
}
.tableHeadingGreen {
    font-weight:700;
    color:green;
    font-size:14px;
}

.tableHeadingLeft {
    font-weight:700;
    text-align:left;
}


.tableHeadingLink {
    font-weight:700;
    color:#5F5F5F;
    text-align:center;
    text-decoration:none;
```

```
}

a:hover.tableHeadingLink {
    font-weight:700;
    color:#5F5F5F;
    text-align:center;
    text-decoration:underline;
}

.tableLink {
    font-weight:200;
    font-size:14px;
    color:#003366;
    text-align:left;
    text-decoration:none;
}

a:hover.tableLink {
    font-weight:200;
    color:#6699cc;
    text-align:left;
    text-decoration:underline;
}

.navigationPage {
    font-size:14px;
    font-weight:700;
    text-align:left;
    color:#003366;
    text-decoration:none;
}

a:hover.navigationPage {
    font-size:14px;
    font-weight:700;
    text-align:left;
    color:#6699cc;
    text-decoration:underline;
}

.emailLink {
    font-weight:200;
    color:#5F5F5F;
    text-align:left;
    text-decoration:underline;
}

a:hover.emailLink {
```

```
    font-weight:200;
    color:#333333;
    text-align:left;
    text-decoration:underline;
}
</style>
</HEAD>


<BODY>


<%

Const APS = "<YOURCMS>"

Const UserID = "<Username>"

Const Password= "<password>"

Const Aut = "secEnterprise"


Function Logon(ByRef IStore)

    Dim SessionManager
    Dim Result
    Result = FALSE
    Set                    SessionManager                    =
Server.CreateObject("CrystalEnterprise.SessionMgr")
    If Err.Number = 0 then
        Dim Sess
        Set    Sess    =    SessionManager.Logon(UserID,
Password, APS, Aut)
        If Err.Number = 0 then
          Set IStore = Sess.Service ("", "InfoStore")
          Set Session("IStore") = IStore
          Result = TRUE
        End If
    end if
   Logon = Result
End Function

Function OpenReport(Report, IStore)
   Dim ReportDoc
   Set                         ReportDoc                      =
Server.CreateObject("CrystalClientDoc.ReportClientDoc
ument")
   ReportDoc.EnterpriseSession                                =
IStore.EnterpriseSession
```

```
   ReportDoc.Open Report
   Set Session("OpenReport") = ReportDoc
   Set OpenReport = ReportDoc
End Function

Function GetAvailableDatabaseTables(ReportDoc)
   Dim pTable
   Dim pTables
   Set                    pTables                    =
Server.CreateObject("CrystalReports.Tables")
     With ReportDoc.Database
        For Each pTable in .Tables
            pTables.Add pTable
        Next
     End With
    Set GetAvailableDatabaseTables = pTables
End Function




Function GetDatabaseInformation(Report)
     With Report.DatabaseController
        Dim CI,Id
        Dim CIs
        Set                        CIs                   =
Report.DatabaseController.GetConnectionInfos(Nothing)
        For Each CI In CIs
            Response.Write("<FONT         color=blue>
UserName: " & CI.UserName & "<BR>")

            For Each Id In CI.Attributes.PropertyIDs

                If                                   (Not
IsObject(CI.Attributes.Item(Id))) Then
                    If (Id = "QE_DatabaseType") Then
                    Response.Write          "Database
Connection Type: " & CI.Attributes.Item(Id) & "<BR>"
                 End if
                if (Id = "QE_ServerDescription") Then
                      Response.Write         "Database
Instance: " & CI.Attributes.Item(Id) & "</FONT><BR>"
                   End If
                Else
                    'The item is another property bag
that you will have to examine.
                End If
```

```
            Next
        Next
    End With

End Function

Function QuerySubreportNames(Report,rname)
     Dim Rptname
     Dim SubCount
     RptName = rname


    Dim SubReportName,STable
    SubCount                                            =
Report.SubreportController.QuerySubreportNames.Count
     If SubCount > 0 then

     For           Each           SubreportName          In
Report.SubreportController.QuerySubreportNames
        Response.Write                           "<BR><FONT
color=#0000CC>Subreport                 </FONT><u><FONT
color=#9900FF>"   &   SubreportName   &   "</FONT></u>
Uses:<BR>"

        For            Each            STable            In
Report.SubreportController.GetSubreportDatabase(Subre
portName).Tables
          if STable.Name <> STable.Alias then
           Response.Write  "<FONT  color=green>  "  &
STable.Name  &  "  Aliased  as  "  &  STable.Alias  &
"</FONT><BR>"
            else
              Response.Write  "<FONT  color=green>  "  &
STable.Name   &   "     and   the   alias   is   the
same</FONT><BR>"
        end if

       Next

        GetDatabaseInformation(Report)
     Next

    else
            Response.Write("<b>" & RptName & "   has
NO Subreports</b>")
   end if


End Function
```

```
Sub PrintForm(AvailableTables)


  Response.Write("<TR><TD>")

    %>


   <%
        Dim pTable
        For Each pTable in AvailableTables
        if pTable.Name <> pTable.Alias then
       Response.Write "<BR>Table Name is <FONT
color=#33CC00> " & pTable.Name & " </FONT>And it is
aliased as:<FONT color=#0099CC> " & pTable.Alias &
"</FONT>"
      else
          Response.Write "<BR>Table Name is <FONT
color=#33CC00> " & pTable.Name & "</FONT> and the
alias is the same"
      end if
        Next
        Response.Write("<BR>")
    %>

    <%

End Sub

Sub Main
   Logon IStore
   Rid = Request.QueryString("ReportID")
   Set Result = IStore.Query("Select SI_ID, SI_NAME,
SI_PARENT_FOLDER From CI_INFOOBJECTS Where SI_ID = "
& Rid)
   Set Report = OpenReport(Result.Item(1),IStore)
   ReportName = Result.Item(1).Title
   Response.Write("<table border=2 width=100%
align=center cellspacing=0 cellpadding=0>")
   Response.Write("<TH style='tableheading'><b>The
Report named<FONT color=red> " & ReportName &
"</FONT> has these tables</TH>")
   Dim Rid,Rname
   Dim IStore, DocManager, Report, ReportName
   Dim Result, AvailableTables,
FieldsOnReport,SubTables

   Set AvailableTables =
GetAvailableDataBaseTables(Report)
```

```
   PrintForm AvailableTables

   GetDatabaseInformation(Report)
  Response.Write("</TABLE>")
  Response.Write("<table     border=2     width=100%
align=center cellspacing=0 cellpadding=0>")
   Response.Write("<TH        style='table'><b><FONT
color=red>" & ReportName   & "  </FONT>has  these
SubReports</TH>")
   Response.Write("<TR><TD style='tablelinkGreen'>")
   QuerySubreportNames Report,ReportName
    Response.Write("</TABLE>")
  End Sub

Main

%>
</BODY>
</HTML>
```

You should be able to check for particular tables by using some variation of these queries and display steps.

Question 81: Division by zero

I have this group:
900 and 600 are sum(current value,terri1)

Here are my values:
territory Id territory Name current prior % change
E01 PC-E01 900 600

I have this formula:
if
sum({@Prior_Contribution},{TRANSACTION_HISTORY.TERR
1}) = 0
then
0
else
100-
(sum({@Prior_Contribution},{TRANSACTION_HISTORY.TER
R1})/sum({@Current_Contribution},{TRANSACTION_HISTOR
Y.TERR1})*100)

I get error division by 0. What could be the problem?

A: This is zero:

sum({@Current_Contribution},{TRANSACTION_HISTORY.TE
RR1})

Change the formula to:

if
sum({@Current_Contribution},{TRANSACTION_HISTORY.TE
RR1} = 0
then
0
else
100-
(sum({@Prior_Contribution},{TRANSACTION_HISTORY.TER
R1})/sum({@Current_Contribution},{TRANSACTION_HISTOR
Y.TERR1})*100)

Question 82: Dollars and cents in ToWords

I have been trying to take a numeric number $48,000.00 and convert it to words. I can do that with the "towords" function. However I have been stuck on getting it to be able to print "Dollars" and "Cents" in the output.

Desired output: One Dollar and xx/36 Cents

This is the formula that I have been working with:
Propercase(ToWords({sys_trac.trackamt})& "Dollars") & " Cents"

I have not been able to get the word "Dollars" to fit correctly.

What is the correct formula for this?

A: This is probably what you want:

```
// Return the cents as words, not fraction:
whileprintingrecords;
numbervar MyValue:= 48900.17;
towords(int(MyValue),0) & " dollars " & towords((MyValue-int(MyValue))*100,0) & " cents"
```

Question 83: Multiple parameters

I need to set up multiple parameters in a report so that the user can decide which parameter they want to use.

For example; the report will have a parameter for account, sales rep, product and state. When they refresh the report, they will see all the available parameters but they will likely only want to run it for one. They might want to run it for sales rep and disregard the rest.

How can I set this up to run so that the remaining parameters can be ignored/left blank?

A: Set default values for each parameter (usually ALL for Text and 0 for numbers) and use your record selection formula to test and use as needed. As an example:

```
(
(If {?param1} = 'ALL' Then
True
Else
{table.sometextfield} = {param1})
)
AND
(
(If {?param2} = 0 Then
True
Else
{table.somenumberfield} = {param2})
)
```

Crystal (especially the later versions) hates blank parameters. Use a default (ALL or 0) to avoid problems and unwanted prompting.

Question 84: Search In multiple fields

I am trying to write a formula so that it searches through multiple fields to find values in address fields. The formula should extract only those that meet the selection. For example:

Fields are say add1, add2, add3 etc

I want to search for the string "CANADA" or "JAPAN"; this could be in upper or lower case. I would also like to may be take the first 3 digit and compare that. How can I achieve this?

A: You can use the record selection formula with a “LIKE” predicate, such as:

```
{table.add1} like "*" + {?MyParameter} + "*"
or
{table.add2} like "*" + {?MyParameter} + "*"
or
{table.add3} like "*" + {?MyParameter} + "*"
```

Question 85: Select non-matching records from two tables

Linking selects records from two tables where there are matching values in the linked fields. This works well for me but I'm having problem with this:

Table 1 and Table 2 (different DBs) both have an indexed field (JobNumber).

I want to select records in Table 1, when no matching record exists in Table 2.

What is the correct formula for this?

A: Use a left join FROM table1 TO table2 and then use a record selection formula like:

isnull({table2.jobnumber})

Question 86: Minimum year selection at a group level

I'm working with Crystal IX using an ODBC connection. I'm pulling records from one table (gifts) where each record could potentially have multiple gifts dates. In trying to determine how many new donors we get each year, I'm referencing the date of donor's first donation.

Example

ID	GiftYear
111	1999
111	2000
111	2001
222	1988
222	1999
333	2000
333	2001
333	2002

I have a grouping on GiftYear and a second grouping on ID and have this formula in my group selection:

Minimum ({@GftYear}, {gifts.patron_id}) = {?parYear}
@GftYear = year({gifts.gift_date})
gifts.patron_id = ID in the above example
?parYear = year(s) the user is asked to enter

When I enter one GiftYear (as in 1988), I get only ID 222 which is exactly as it should be.

However when I enter 1999 and 2000 for GiftYear, it gives me ID 111 under 1999 (as it should be) but it also lists it under year 2000 in addition to ID 333, thereby incorrectly indicating two donors gave for the first time in 2000.

Eventually, I would need to get total number of donors, amount donated and average donation for each year. What is the correct method to do what I need?

A: The problem you are running into is that the use of a group on year forces your group selection only to apply to that year, since the client ID group is nested within it. Go to database->database expert->your datasource->add command and enter something like:

```
Select gifts.`ID`, min(gifts.`giftdate`) as mindate
From `gifts` gifts
Group by gifts.`ID`
```

Then link the command to the gifts table on ID and on giftdate, and for link options, choose "enforce both". This will cause the main report only to return the first giftdate. You can then use mindate in your year formula.

If possible, set up the entire query as a command for speed in which case you would accomplish the above a little differently, setting up the minimum date in the where clause like this:

```
where gifts.`giftdate` = (select min(A.`giftdate`) from gifts A where A.`ID` = gifts.`ID`)
```

Question 87: String manipulation

I have a name field in my report that pulls the clients name from the database like this "Doe, John". How can I display only the Last name?

A: Try a formula like this:

```
left({table.name},instr({table.name},",")-1)
```

Question 88: Record selection

I need to report only patient records that contain services dates prior to 11/2006 but current patients are also being seen in 6/2007.

I'm grouping by patient number like:

Patient #	Date of Service
146097	3/2006
	7/2006
	4/2007
	6/2007
186221	2/2007
	6/2007
223733	8/2006
	12/2006
	4/2007
	6/2007

With this sample data, what I should have is just the listing of 146097 and 223733. What am I missing?

A: A different approach would be to insert a group on patientID and then go to report; >selection formula->GROUP and enter:

```
minimum({table.date},{table.patientID}) < date(2006,11,1) and
maximum({table.date},{table.patientID}) >= date(2007,6,1) and
maximum({table.date},{table.patientID}) < date(2007,7,1)
```

If you just want the most recent date to be anytime after 6/1, then remove the last clause.

Question 89: Sorting on Alpha and Numeric using parameters

I have designed a report that produces a list that I would like to sort on the persons name or the value of their loan balances.

I can do this using the record sort expert but I would like to give the user the option to choose.

I can create a parameter and the use the result in a formula field to sort on like:

if {?Sortby} = "Name" then {@ContractorName} else {@LoanBalance}

However, as the name is alpha and the loan numeric, the formula is rejected.

I've tried converting the loan 'ToText' but ran into many problems especially as there are some negative values too. Can this be done?

A: Usually that cannot be done as you have found, but maybe this:

```
CODE:
if {?Sortby} = "Name" then
 AscW({@ContractorName})
else {@LoanBalance}
```

This converts the name into a Number (the ASCII (Unicode) value of the string). It should sort as expected.

Another approach would be to create two formulas and add them as sort fields:

if {?Sort by} = "Name" then {@Contractor's Name}

if {?Sort by} = "Balance" then {@LoanBalance}

If the option is not selected, the formulas will default to "" or 0 respectively and have no impact on the sort.

Question 90: Setting specified date

I want to make my report run from every Wednesday to Wednesday. It consists of this:

{HPD_HelpDesk.Create Time} >= CurrentDate-7

and

time({HPD_HelpDesk.Create Time}) in time(16,0,0) to time(23,59,59)

But I want to set up such that it runs every Wednesday to Wednesday. How can I do that?

A: Maybe you mean from Wednesday through Tuesday. This depends upon when you plan to run the report. The following formula would work for the Wednesday from the previous week to the Tuesday of the current week:

{HPD_HelpDesk.Create Time} in CurrentDate-dayofweek(currentdate)-3 to CurrentDate-dayofweek(currentdate)+ 3 and
time({HPD_HelpDesk.Create Time}) in time(16,0,0) to time(23,59,59)

Question 91: Page header showing on graph page

I have a report with detailed data and then a graph on the group header (grouped by product) so I can see a graph for each product. The problem is that the column headers that are in the page header section show up on pages that have just the graph as well as pages with the data.

Is there a way to have the column headers only show for the detailed data?

A: You can use the page header for the column labels (remove GH_a so that your charts are in the first group header section). Create two formulas:

//{@false} to be placed in the report header and in the detail section:
whileprintingrecords;
booleanvar flag := false;

//{@true} to be placed in the group header containing the charts:
whileprintingrecords;
booleanvar flag := true;

Then go to the section expert->page header->suppress->x+2 and enter:

whileprintingrecords;
booleanvar flag;
flag = true //note no colon

You can suppress the formulas so they don't show.

Question 92: Null out formula if field is blank

I have two formulas:

f_One: '<b>Desc: </b>'
f_Two: {Table1.Field1}

I place these fields onto my report in Details c:

f_One f_Two

Details c is set to Suppress Blank Section.

What I would like to do is if f_Two is Null, make f_One Null so that Details c would be suppressed for that record. I can't combine both formulas into one because f_Two has to line up with the previous rows column. Can this be done?

A: Right click on the first formula->Format field->suppress->x+2 and enter:

isnull({table1.field1})

Then make sure the section is formatted to "suppress blank section".

Question 93: Displaying non existing sub group

I have 2 sets of subgroups that I want to display to my report for all main groups that exist. My report will only display the subgroup that has a record.

How can I display all the sub groups in my report even if there is only one sub group with records?

A: This is a common problem with Crystal. It's designed on the assumption you don't want to see a possible group with no items in it. If you do, there are various work-rounds.

The best solution is to create a table for each category and then link it using a left-outer to link to the details. This depends on you being allowed to create a new table or can easily get one created to your specifications.

Another solution is to create running totals for both groups. Put each running total in a different section of the report footer. Suppress that section when the total is greater than zero so only omitted groups are mentioned. It must be the report footer because running totals are accumulated during the course of the run.

Question 94: Display group message based on a field value

I have a report that I have grouped on a field called userdef4. The userdef 4 is either null or "Y". This generates a report with the top set of records which are marked "Y" and the bottom group which are "null" in userdef4. I would like a message to print above the group of item(s) that are null in userdef4. Can this be done in CR?

Example:
Report Title
userdef4 = "Y" *** No message if userdef4 is "Y"***
 item 1
 item 2
 item 3

userdef4 = null *** Message if userdef4 is null***
 item 4
 item 5

A: Create a formula in the formula editor (field explorer->formula->new):

```
if isnull({table.userdef4}) then
"Your message"
```

Place this formula in the group header.

Question 95: Shared NumberVar double-counting last record in group

I am using a Shared NumberVAR formula to total outstanding bills by location based on how long they've been outstanding and whether they are overdue or not. I can't use a running total or simple Sum of Field to get the result I want because the database is very normalized and the bill can be paid in installments so I need to look at various levels of data to know whether to count the amount as outstanding or not.

I have one copy of the formula in the Detail level of the report, which adds up fine for each valid record but when I place a copy of the formula in the Group footer, if the last record at detail level, was counted in the shared numbervar, then its added again in the group footer making the final result wrong.

Is there a formula to do this?

A: You shouldn't be putting the calculation formula in the group footer. Let's say your calculation formula looks like:

```
whileprintingrecords;
shared numbervar x := x + {table.amt};
```

The group footer formula, to display the result, should read:

```
whileprintingrecords;
shared numbervar x;
```

If instead you place the calculation formula in the group footer, it will add the last detail value again.

Question 96: Date range check

I have two dates; one for check out and one for check in. The dates are written as date/time to capture the exact time a check out or check in occurred.

I am comparing this to a range of dates from a different table that stores all date/times as the date and 12:00am as the time.

This is how I am determining if my trans_date is within the check out - check in range:

```
if {WIP_LABOR_BOOKING.TRANS_DATE} in
{TC_CKO_CKIN_DETAIL_VW.CHECK_OUT_DATE}
to {TC_CKO_CKIN_DETAIL_VW.CHECK_IN_DATE} then
"YES" else "NO"
```

The problem is that the Trans_Date is the one with the 12:00am time on all the dates so any Check_Out or Check_in with the same date and (for example) 3:00 pm as the time, would not put the Trans_date in the range of the check-out or Check_in.

How can I check the range only using the date criteria and excluding the time?

A: Try this formula:

```
if Date({WIP_LABOR_BOOKING.TRANS_DATE}) in
date({TC_CKO_CKIN_DETAIL_VW.CHECK_OUT_DATE})
to date({TC_CKO_CKIN_DETAIL_VW.CHECK_IN_DATE})
then "YES" else "NO"
```

Question 97: CrossTab grouping daily, weekly, monthly

I have a parameter driven report that asks a user if they want daily (rolling 8 days), weekly (rolling 8 weeks) or monthly (rolling 8 months) worth of data. Based on the parameter entered the Crosstab should group by days, weeks or months.

Data retrieved from the database is by days.
As an example: daily should show:

```
  05/13 05/14 05/15 .... 05/21
A  10     0    20      15
B  5     10    15       2
```

Weekly should show:

```
  03/26 04/02 04/09 .... 05/14
A  20     0    25      15
B  10    15    25       4
```

Monthly should show:

```
  09/2006 10/2006 11/2006 .... 04/2007
A  100      0      200       150
B  50      110     151       200
```

I can put the same crosstab in subsections a, b, c one for daily, one for weekly and one for monthly and suppress the ones not selected. Is there a way to write a formula so I can have only one crosstab?

A: Create a formula like this:

```
select {?period}
case "daily" : {table.date}
case "weekly" : {table.date}-dayofweek({table.date})+1
case "monthly" : {table.date}-day({table.date})+1
```

Use this formula for your column field.

Question 98: Calculate all weeks that begin in the same month

I am creating a report that will run weekly (Sunday - Saturday) showing records that were opened in the prior week/month.

For example: for the month of July 2007, this would include data for weeks beginning July 1, July 8, July 15, July 22, and July 29. So the week of July 29 will contain data through August 4.

The report is currently grouped by week based on open date as seen below:

12/31/2006 3
1/7/2007 4
1/14/2007 6
1/21/2007 5
1/28/2007 11
2/4/2007 10
2/11/2007 15
2/18/2007 3
2/25/2007 5
3/4/2007 9
3/11/2007 10
3/18/2007 5
3/25/2007 12

Is there a formula that will sum all the weeks that begin in the same month?

A: Try something like:

```
if month({table.date}-dayofweek({table.date})+1) =
month(currentdate-
day(currentdate)) then {table.amt}
```

Insert summaries on this formula.

Question 99: Cross-tab effect with summary fields

I am working with a client database and pulling from 2 tables. The first is service_records and that gives me the client_id and service_number. I've got it joined (left-inner) to the assessment_table on client_id and service_number so it returns the date_of_assessment.

What this returns is any instance where there is a service number and the date_of_assessment (if there is any). If there wasn't an assessment given at all, it returns the service_number with a Null value for date_of_assessment. If more than one assessment was given for that service_number, it returns one line for each assessment given. I've also got a formula field that calculates the days since the assessment and another that takes that result and categorizes that record into "0-90 days", "91-180", "181 days +", and "no assessment". Here's an example minus the formula fields:

Client_ID Service_Number Date_of_assessment
Location

1310 12
Detroit
1311 6 4/1/2007
Miami
1311 6 1/2/2007
Miami
1311 6 8/15/2006
Miami

I then group by client_id and have the most recent assessment given, the days since that assessment and the category in the header. All I'm really interested in is the last assessment.

What I want to do is have a cross-tab (or something that looks like one) that counts patients that fall into each category for each location. How I went about this was to Put the location in rows and the categories in columns and then do a distinct count on client_id. The trouble I am running into is that I only want to count records that show up in the group header. What I am getting is, if there is a client who was given an assessment 80 days ago and one 120 days ago, it counts that client in each category.

How do I construct a tab that will summarize this data but count only the records that show up in my group header?

A: You need to set up a command that will return either a null or the most recent date of assessment. Make a new blank report->datasource->add command and enter something like this:

```
SELECT `Service_Records`.`Client_ID`,
`Service_Records`.`Service_Number`,
`Assessment_Table`.`Location`,`Assessment_Table`.`Client_I
D`,
`Assessment_Table`.`Date_of_Assessment`
FROM `Service_Records` `Service_Records`
LEFT OUTER JOIN `Assessment_Table` `Assessment_Table`
ON
`Service_Records`.`Client_ID`=`Assessment_Table`.`Client_I
D` and
`Service_Records`.`Service_Number` =
`Assessment_Table`.`Service_Number`
 WHERE
(
`Assessment_Table`.`Date_of_Assessment` is null or
`Assessment_Table`.`Date_of_Assessment` = (select
max(A.`Date_of_Assessment`)
from Assessment_Table A, Service_Records B where
B.`Client_ID` = Service_Records.`Client_ID` and
A.`Client_ID` = B.`Client_ID`
)
)
 ORDER BY `Service_Records`.`Client_ID`
```

This will return one row per Client ID. You will then be able to insert the crosstab and get the desired results.

Question 100: Exclude patient records who get a particular service

Where I work, clients get a variety of services. If I returned all the service records for a group of clients, it might look something like this:

Client_id	Service_number	Service_code
100	1	IP
100	2	SC
100	3	MM
100	4	OU
200	1	SC
200	2	MM
200	3	OC
300	1	GH
300	2	SC
300	3	MM

I want all the records for clients who don't get particular service types - in this case "IP" and "GH". How do I write a command line that will look at each client to see if they get those services and then return the client records for those that don't?

After the query, the above data should look like this:

Client_id	Service_number	Service_code
200	1	SC
200	2	MM
200	3	OC

Client 100 should be excluded b/c he receives service "IP" and client 300 should be excluded b/c he gets "GH".

A: An easy way to handle this is to create a formula {@hascode} in the field explorer of CR:

if {table.service_code} in ["IP","GH"] then 1 else 0

Do not use record selection criteria on the codes field. Instead, insert a group on {table.clientID} and then go to report->selection formula->GROUP and enter:

sum({@hascode},{table.clientID}) = 0

This will return all records for clients who don't have IP or GH in any of their records. You could replace the hard codes in your original formula to use a parameter with multiple values:

if {table.service_code} = {?Code} then 1 else 0

Note that if you then need to summarize across clients, you will need to use running totals, since inserted summaries would still evaluate the non-group selected records. Running totals, on the other hand, only pick up on the group-selected records.

Question 101: Conditionally displaying grouped data

I have a report where I need to display certain fields depending on criteria applicable to the project.

If the project has benchmarking applied to it, I need to display only the benchmarking fields.

If a project has market testing applied to it, I need to display only the market testing fields

If a project has market testing & benchmarking, I need to display both benchmarking and market testing fields.

How can I put these fields into groups but need to only display those groups appropriate to the project?

A: Go to the section expert and click the formula button next to the suppress tick box. The formula window will then appear. You need something like:

{tablename.field} = 'What_ever_your_condition_is'

Question 102: Page break in a sub report

We print invoices and the bottom third of page one is a tear off remittance slip. A sub report begins printing details of the invoice starting on page two (back side of page one - we print the invoices duplex). We don't want the bottom third of the back of page one to have anything printed on it because it will be on the back side of the remittance slip.

How can we cause the sub report to force a page break after printing five detail rows in this sub report?

A: In the sub report, insert a running total {#cnt} that does a count of any recurring field, evaluate for each record, reset never. Then go to the section expert within the subreport->details->new page after and enter:

{#cnt} = 5

This assumes that you only need the page break once.

Another formula used in the detail of the subreport is (recordcount mod 5)= 0 .

Question 103: Count the number of dates in a group

I have generated a report that has four items in the details section: CustomerID, Service Type, Start Date, and End Date. For some records, there is no end date as services are ongoing. I want to have a summary field in a group that counts the number of closed services (wherever an end-date shows up). I tried to use a summary field and count but it counts instances where there is no date. How do I write a formula or a custom summary that will only count when there is an occurrence of a date?

A: Do a running total of:

```
count->date
reset->group
evaluate->use a formula:

not(isnull({table.date}))
and
{table.date} <> cdate(0,0,0)
```

Question 104: Display "No records" when there are none

I run a report everyday and sometimes there are no records because there isn't any that match my criteria. What I would like to do is display the message "no records today" when there are none. How can I do this?

A: Insert another page header section below the one that includes your column headings. Then go to the field explorer->formulas->new and enter:

if isnull({table.field}) then
"No records today"

Make sure that the field you use in the formula is recurring, i.e., that it always is populated when the report returns any records. Place this formula in page header_b. Then go into the section expert->page header_b->check "suppress blank section".

For this to work you must also go to file->report options and make sure that the following is NOT checked: "Suppress Printing if No Records".

Question 105: Rounding in crosstab

I'm using a CRXI R2. I have a crosstab that shows a Distinct Count of a field as the summary. I use the same Distinct Count field in the summary but as a percentage which is underneath it. It looks great, but it always adds up to 99% instead of 100%.

I realize it's a rounding issue, so I Right Click on the cell, Format Fields and change the Rounding to ".01". When I click OK, nothing changes. If I go back into Format Fields, Crystal put it back to Rounding "1".

How should I handle this?

A: You can handle this by doing the following:

Remove your current percentage summary in the crosstab and instead create a formula like the following and add it as your second summary (Note that you must have a group on your row field in the main report, even if the group sections are suppressed):

```
distinctcount({table.summaryfield},{table.rowfield})
```

Then change the summary to a maximum so that the same row total value appears in each cell of a specific row.

Next select your first summary for both inner cells and subtotal and total cells all at once->right click->format field->common tab->suppress->x+2 and enter:

```
whileprintingrecords;
numbervar curr := currentfieldvalue;
false
```

Then select the formula summary for both inner cells and subtotal and total cells all at once->->right click->format field->common tab->suppress->x+2 and enter:

```
whileprintingrecords;
numbervar tot := currentfieldvalue;
false
```

Then in the same common tab->display string->x+2 and enter:

```
whileprintingrecords;
numbervar curr;
numbervar tot;
if tot <> 0 then
totext(curr%tot,2)+"%" //for two decimals
```

Question 106: Formula using variables

I am using CR XI. I have a SQL query that returns summed up values (4 rows to be exact)

```
Item   Sum
----   ---
A      10
B      20
C      40
D       5
```

I have to show these values up on the report header. So I have created formulas with variables that store these values. The formula is:

```
WhilePrintingRecords;
NumberVar TotalA:= 0;

While not OnLastRecord
Do

  If {Command.Item} = 'A'
  Then TotalA := TotalA + {Command.Sum}
```

I was planning to do the same for each Item (A, B,C, D) but this formula is throwing an error "A loop was evaluated more than the maximum number of times allowed".

How do I work around this issue?

A: You won't be able to loop through all the records in one run of a formula.

I would suggest creating four formulas, one for each Item type:

```
//@Item_A
if {Command.Item} = "A"
then {Command.Sum}
else 0

//@Item_B
```

```
if {Command.Item} = "B"
then {Command.Sum}
else 0

//@Item_C
if {Command.Item} = "C"
then {Command.Sum}
else 0

//@Item_D
if {Command.Item} = "D"
then {Command.Sum}
else 0
```

You can then insert a summary field off each formula and place them in the report header.

CRYSTAL REPORT: General Issues

Question 107: Crystal

Does crystal build the query and then pass it to the database to generate the query?

A: If you're using Crystal and SQL, then you'll see the SQL generated by choosing Database > Show SQL. That is just the part that the report sends to the server, it may do extra selection on what the server returns.

Crystal then groups / sorts the records, then prints them, these are distinct processes.

Crystal is a reporting tool that allows you to produce neat-looking reports very quickly. It isn't a full programming language though it does include a lot of options that you can control in a subtle way.

Question 108: Help with selection

I have a report that uses two tables, one table has customer orders and one has cancelled customer orders. So if an order is placed, an entry goes into table1. If this order is then cancelled an entry goes into table2, the entry in table1 is unaffected. The tables are linked by an order number.

The report lists all orders taken by a user but includes cancelled ones, how do I exclude these from the report?

A: Make sure that the join is a Left Outer join.

Then in the Report->Selection Formula->Record place:

isnull({table2.orderid})

Question 109: Cross tab report

Can we attach an on-demand sub report to a cross tab report?

A: Sub reports do not "attach" to crosstabs.

Create the crosstab manually using groups and aggregates and then link the subreport by the appropriate group.

Question 110: Create a custom paper size form

How do you create a custom paper size form to display or print a report with a predefined custom paper size for use in Crystal Reports?

A: To create a custom paper size form, complete the applicable steps for the environment you are working in. Before you begin, you must be sure that the printer driver is able to support printing a custom size paper.

- Each printer driver produces a different display for printer layout options. If the printer driver selected has the functionality to be customized, you will be able to select the Custom Paper icon or the Custom button. Selecting the Custom button enables you to set the height and width of the paper size form.
- Creating a report with a custom paper size on one computer and then attempting to print the report on a different computer with the customized paper size form may produce different results.

If Crystal Reports is installed on a Windows 2000 or NT computer, complete the following steps:

1. Click Start > Settings > Control Panel.
2. Double-click Printers, click File > Server Properties > Create a new form (in the Forms tab)
3. Type a name such as "CustomPaperForm" in Form Name.
4. Select Metric to use centimeters or select English to use inches for the Units under the Form description section.
5. Enter the Height and Width under the Paper size section.
6. Enter the Left, Right, Top, and Bottom margins under the Printer area margins section.
7. Click Save form and then click OK.

To apply the custom paper size form, complete the following:

1. Launch Crystal Reports, and select the report.
2. Click File and click Printer Setup.
3. Select the custom paper size form from Paper.

If Crystal Reports is installed on a Windows 9.x or ME computer, complete the following steps:

1. Launch Crystal Reports, and select the report.
2. Click File > Printer Setup > Properties.
3. Click Custom, and then click the Custom button.
4. Enter the custom height and width of the paper.
5. Click OK.

Question 111: Show/Hide Group Tree defaults

I'm using CR/CE 10 with an Oracle db. Reports in Crystal format are by default showing the Group tree. My users never use it so it's just taking up space on their monitors and every time they open a report, the first thing they do is click on the icon to hide this. Is there a way to automatically hide the Group Tree?

A: There is a setting under the Web Component Server to turn the Group Tree off.

Go to the CMC, Servers, Crystal Web Component Server and on the Properties tab you will see an option "Hide the Group Tree (if it is displayed)"

The other way you can do it is in each report, under File, Report Options, set the Show Group Tree to off. Then republish the report.

Question 112: Error since upgrading to BOXI R2

"An error occurred at the server: Your request was refused because you do not have the right 'Download files associated with the report' on report 'Report Name'. Please ask your system administrator to grant you this right"

This error happens when a user tries to export to Crystal Report format from a Crystal Report so they can save it on their desktop in CR format. It appears I have to give each user the 'Download files associated with the report right'.

Is there any way to make this right associated with all users or do I have to give this right on every report?

A: You can set the group's rights to allow this in each folder, where needed - not needed to be set on each report in that folder. Have a look in the CMC under Business Objects Applications under Infoview to see if the download rights can be set for each group there.
It is in the Advanced Rights page of the CMC, under the "Report" section (which isn't visible by default so you'll need to expand it).

Question 113: Infoview Error

When I log in as a user to Infoview, I receive the following error: An error has occurred: No 508 compliant <TITLE> found in resource strings.

What is causing this error?

A: The problem you are seeing is caused by Version 2.0 .NET framework being installed on your server.

Crystal Reports Server and Business Objects Enterprise XI require .NET Framework version 1.1.4322 whereas your server probably has .NET Framework version 2.0 installed. These 2 (and other) versions of .NET Framework can coexist on the one server, however they need to be installed in a "side-by-side installation".

There are 2 solutions:

1. When attempting to view a report in InfoView, the following error message appears:

"An error has occurred: No 508 compliant...found in resource strings"
Cause

This message occurs because the businessobjects virtual directory in Internet Information Server (IIS) is set to use 2.0 version of the .NET framework. BusinessObjects Enterprise XI only supports version 1.1 of the .NET framework.

To resolve this error message do the following:

a. Go to Start > Settings > Control Panel > Administrative Tools > Internet Services Manager.
b. Expand the objects tree for the IIS Server > Web Sites > Default Web Site.
c. Right-click the businessobjects virtual directory and choose Properties from the context menu.
d. Select the ASP.NET tab.

e. Using the drop down box change the version from 2.0.50727 to 1.1.4322. Note your point versions may not match these exactly; the essential version is 1.1x and not 2.x.
f. Click the OK button to save your changes.
g. Repeat steps 3 through 6 for the crystalreportviewers11 virtual directory.
h. Click Start, click Run, and type "iisreset" to shut down and restart IIS.

If the virtual directory version of the ASP.NET framework and your Internet Information Server does not list version 1.1x then do the following:

a. Uninstall version 2.0 of the .NET Framework
b. Reinstall version 1.1.
c. To install version 2.0 of the .NET Framework in a side-by-side configuration without updating ASP .NET click Start, click Run, and use the following switches:

dotnetfx.exe /c:"install /noaspupgrade /l /q"

2. Add a new Web Service Extension to IIS for .NET Framework v 1.1.4322, if you are running IIS6 and have Microsoft.NET v1.1.4322 already installed

Question 114: Using group calculation in report totals

I am using CR 11.5. I am linking two files together. The first file contains estimated (accrued) freight related to customer shipments. The second file contains the payments made to freight vendors that relate to the accruals in the first file. There can be multiple payments on file 2 for each estimate on file 1. The records on the two files are linked via a reconciliation-code. For example:

File 1

Rec-Cd	SlsInv#	Est$
1	100	2000
3	250	1500
4	300	750

File 2

Rec-Cd	VdrInv#	Pmt$
1	123	1800
1	125	200
3	253	1400

The files are left outer joined on File 1 (because some estimates have no payments yet). The results look as follows.

Rec-Cd	SlsInv#	Est$	VdrInv#	Pmt$
1	100	2000	123	1800
1	100	2000	125	200
3	250	1500	253	1400
4	300	750	-	-

I am grouping by Rec-Cd. Within this group I average Est$, sum Pmt$ and calculate the balance as the difference. This gives me the correct data at the Rec-Cd level (1 is zero, 3 is 100, etc.).

How do I then sum these balances at the vendor or report total? The calculated Balance field is not available for further calculations.

A: You could do this at least in two different ways. You could have used a running total instead of an average that evaluated on change of rec_cd, reset on change of rec-cd, with a separate running total for the vendor level (reset on change of vendor), and at the report level with no reset. Then you could use those in three different formulas.

Or you can continue on your current path, and create variables to handle the vendor and report totals, and this requires four formulas:

```
//{@resetvendor} to be placed in the vendor group header:
whileprintingrecords;
numbervar vdrbal;
if not inrepeatedgroupheader then
vdrdbal := 0;

//{@accum} to be placed in the rec_cd group header or footer:
whileprintingrecords;
numbervar vdrbal := vdrbal +
average({table.est$},{table.rec_cd}) -
sum({table.pmt$},{table.rec_cd});
numbervar rptbal := rptbal +
average({table.est$},{table.rec_cd}) -
sum({table.pmt$},{table.rec_cd});

//{@displvdrbal} to be placed in the vendor group footer:
whileprintingrecords;
numbervar vdrbal;

//{@displrptbal} to be placed in the report footer:
whileprintingrecords;
numbervar rptbal;
```

If your est$ and pmt$ fields are of currency datatype, change "numbervar" to "currencyvar" in all formulas.

Question 115: Split address fields

I have to split address fields such as 101 maple street #211 or 202 wall ave. Apt 209 into street number, street name and apt number separately. How can I do that in CRXI?

A: Treat the elements as separate fields, Split({address1}, " ")[1] and so on.
For an address like 10 NEW ROAD, "10" would be element [1], "NEW" would be element [2], "ROAD" would be element [3] and element [4] would be null. Put them in formula fields and adjust them there. Remember that formulas stop when they hit a null, unless ISNULL is used to test.

You can also use UBOUND to find the number of table elements.

```
//for {@element2}:
if ubound(split({your.field},":")) >= 2 then
split({your.field},":")[2]

//for {@element3}:
if ubound(split({your.field},":")) >= 3 then
split({your.field},":")[3]
```

In your case, the apartment and its variable indicator make for extra problems. If it is always the last element, you could get it using unbound to find which the last is. If number is always the first and street name is in the middle, you could clear the extras from 'Street Name' by taking the middle elements, putting them into a single formula field and then using Replace to get rid of things like #, comma, full stop and "Apt".

Question 116: Group totals as parameters for subreports

I'm trying to get individual counts of the total number of site records in four separate geographical areas in the main report and then use them for calculations in subreports for example, the subreport I'm most concerned with shows only the sites which have downtime records associated to them but I'd like to be able to compare these downtime records to the total number of sites in their respective areas to calculate network availability by area.

I want create these four individual counts by area and then pass them separately to the subreport but I'm only able to pass the grand total. Would the best way to separate these is by using the report footer(s) then?

A: You can't pass data upwards from the main report to the sub, since you have to use shared variables which occurs whileprintingrecords. Why are you linking the sub? You wouldn't actually set the values up as a parameter, although you could link on other parameters, e.g., if you wanted to define the same time period in both main and sub.

You should either move the subreports to the report footer, or insert another report header section_a to hold a subreport that calculates the group values for the entire areas. Let's say you choose to do the latter. In the new sub in RH_a, create a formula like the following and place it in the area group header:

```
whileprintingrecords;
shared numbervar array dcntsite;
shared stringvar array area;
numbervar cnt := cnt + 1;

if cnt < 1000 then (
redim preserve dcntsite[cnt];
dcntsite[cnt] := distinctcount({table.site},{table.area});
redim preserve area[cnt];
area[cnt] := {table.area}
);
```

Then in the subreport in RH_b, create a formula:

```
whileprintingrecords;
shared numbervar array dcntsite;
shared stringvar array area;
numbervar tot;
numbervar i;

for i := 1 to ubound(dcntsite) do (
if area[i] = {table.area} then
tot := dcntsite[i]
);
tot
```

You can do a calculation right in this formula or you can reference tot in another formula, e.g.:

```
whileprintingrecords;
numbervar tot;
distinctcount({table.site},{table.area})%tot
```

Question 117: Running totals in a Cross-Tab

I have Running Totals which I use in a Cross Tab in CRXI. When I try to calculate percentage from these 2 Running Totals, I get an error message:

"A Print Time formula that modifies variables is used in a cart or a map Details: @% G1OnTime"

The Cross Tab Structure is as follows:

Rows: - Different Support Teams (database field)
Column 1 : Tickets Due (Running Total)
Column 2 : Tickets within Commit Date (Running Total)
Column 3 : Ontime % (Column 2/Column 1 * 100)

I can't include Column 3 in my Cross Tab on which I get the above error message. Are there any workarounds or other ways to get the overall percentage of Running Totals?

A: Add the first two summaries to the crosstab and then create a formula to add as the third summary:

```
whilereadingrecords;
0
```

Then in preview mode, select the first summary->right click->format field->suppress->x+2 and enter:

```
whileprintingrecords;
numbervar tickdue := currentfieldvalue;
false
```

Then select the second summary->right click->format field->suppress->x+2 and enter:

```
whileprintingrecords;
numbervar tickintime := currentfieldvalue;
false
```

Finally, select the third summary->right click->format field->DISPLAY STRING->x+2 and enter:

```
whileprintingrecords;
numbervar tickdue;
numbervar tickintime;
if tickdue <> 0 then
totext(tickintime%tickdue,2)+"%" //2 is the number of decimals
```

Question 118: Large crosstab

I have a very large cross-tab in CR10 that is causing me some problems. The cross-tab itself is located in a subreport in a group header on the main report. The cross-tab is set up to fill a square in black when the column total is > 1, creating a "true" condition. If the column total = 0 or "false" the field is blank. It's a visual grid representing scientific samples and what analyses need to be performed on any given sample.

The problem is that it can potentially have a lot of rows and columns. Several things are happening at the moment. In this specific data set, the rows are at 61 records and the there are 52 records in the column field. As expected, the columns are spilling over to the "virtual pages", 3 of them to be exact and the rows are also going to 3 pages. The problem is that the virtual pages aren't printing or showing up when I preview the entire report, only the subreport. It seems to be working properly until it gets to row 61 when it repeats rows 1-61 but with the exact same columns, 1-17 rather than 17-34.

Ideally, what I'd like to do is display rows 1-18, with columns 1-17 on the first page. Page 2 would then be rows 19-39, columns 1-17, page 3 rows 40-61 with columns 1-17. The next page should now repeat rows 1-18 but with columns 17-34 and so on.

Is there a better way to deal with this data?

A: The problem is the use of a subreport which doesn't expand to virtual pages. If you placed the crosstab directly into the report, you shouldn't have a problem. If you place it in the report footer, you will have page footer where you can place a page number and a horizontal page number for assembling when you print. Note that virtual pages print first, so the numbering would be: page 1-1, page 1-2, page 1-3, page 2-1, page 2-2, etc., where the second number is the horizontal page number.

Question 119: Run on demand subreport at drilldown

I'm designing a report in CRIX. The main report has several groups with total fields and a hidden detail section. The detail section contains a subreport that I would like to execute on drilldown. If I just insert a subreport in the hidden detail section it gets executed on each pass of data making for a slow report. If I place an ondemand subreport in hidden detail section then users have to click twice, once to drilldown into details and again to click on the ondemand subreport.

Is there a way to execute subreport in a hidden detail section when I double-click to drilldown to details of main report?

A: Instead of hiding the section containing the subreport (not on-demand), suppress the section with a conditional formula:

drilldowngrouplevel = 0

This will return only the records in the main report until you drilldown.

Question 120: Using "Count" to find a weekly average

I am creating a dash board and I need to get an "average" on a weekly "count" of work orders. It will not allow me to use a count to determine an average of Work Orders from the beginning of the year. I have tried to convert the count to a number variable thinking that might enable me to get an average but again I get the same error message. I am using Crystal Reports 10.

MSToShop
((Count({TWORK_ORDER.WO_ID},{TWORK_ORDER.DATE_RELEASED},"weekly")));

AvgToShop
Average((ToNumber({@MSToShop})),{TWORK_ORDER.DATE_RELEASED},"YearToDate");

The "(ToNumber({@MSToShop}))" is highlighted when I run the check and it says "A field is required here." How should I handle this?

A: I think you would have to handle this with a variable. If you have your report set up with a weekly group, then you have to create a formula like this to be placed in the week group header or footer:

//{@accum}: whileprintingrecords; numbervar sumcnt := sumcnt + count({TWORK_ORDER.WO_ID},{TWORK_ORDER.DATE_RELEASED},"weekly"); numbervar cnt := cnt + 1;

Then in the report footer use a formula like this to display the average:

```
whileprintingrecords;
numbervar sumcnt;
numbervar cnt;
sumcnt/cnt
```

Question 121: Subreport performance consideration

I have main report spread over 3000 pages by agent numbers. I added two subreports over agent number group header. The report start accessing database, reading subreport records every time I click next page. Is this normal due to subreport?

A: The subreports will execute every time there is a new group, assuming they are linked on the groupfield. If you want the subs to execute when you first run the report (not just when paging through it), then add page N of M to the page footer. This will force the execution of all subreports when you run the report.

Question 122: Page Number with subreports

I have 6 different reports and I need to make the 7th include the 6 reports.

All the subreports are in the RF of the global report. I have two problems:

1. The page number is not visible in the global report.
2. I am using the condition New Page After for each subreport and when the subreport is empty, I get a blank page (I was setting the option for the blank report).

Is there a way to print the number page on the global report?

A: Make sure the page number is in the page footer and not in the report footer.

Select each subreport->format subreport->subreport tab->check "suppress blank subreport". In the main report, go into the section expert and check "suppress blank section" for each section containing a subreport.

Question 123: Share data between two subreports

I have a continuing problem: Our invoices need to skip printing on the bottom third of the back of the first page since that is the back of the tear off coupon that gets sent back with payment.

We have two sub reports that print on the back of the first page. The first approach I tried was to just count lines in the first sub report and cause a page break at the appropriate count.

Unfortunately, half the time we don't reach the line limit and another sub report starts printing. The second sub report overflows onto the back of the remittance coupon.

Can I share the row count between sub reports?

A: **Yes, if you set the count up as a shared variable in each subreport.**

Question 124: Supress subreport during drill down on main report

I'm using crystal 10 connected to a sql server 2000 database via ODBC.

I have a report with a split report footer (a and b) which contains a subreport placed in report footer b. This subreport is an almost identical copy of the main report, except that different criteria are used for evaluating certain formulae. The problem I have encountered is that if I drill down on a record in the main report and then skip ahead a page or two, I can still see the whole of the subreport which shouldn't be visible at this level as it would be confusing to the users. Is there any way of telling crystal that I want to suppress the subreport, or report footer b, if I am looking at a drill down in the main report?

A: Go to the section expert->RF_b->suppress->x+2 and enter:

drilldowngrouplevel > 0

where 0 represents no drilldown, 1 = first drilldown, etc.

Question 125: Limitations of Crystal Preview

I have Crystal XI R2 Professional as do the users of my reports.

The problem I have is that when they use the "Preview" function, and double click a drillable field, sometimes they accidently move an object and skew the view. Also, the Preview mode includes much of the menus taking up too much valuable screen space just to navigate the results of a report. I tried to find some kind of "Lock" function such as something MS Word has to lock the fields in place and prevent any changes, but couldn't find anything. I do have the report file as read only so they can't permanently mess up the file, but it still is a pain for the users when they do make a change accidently in Preview mode. And hiding menu's helps, but it still seems there should be a "lighter" version that maximizes screen space.

I would like to know if there is a crystal viewer that is included with Crystal XI that will allow users to refresh a report (putting in new prompts), drill the data, and not be able to actually edit the report in anyway. If there is, where can I get find this viewer?

A: Most fields should have an option on the Format>Common tab to lock position and size. I use this often when designing reports so that I don't move things around.

Question 126: Speed differences between Views and Stored Procedures

In my crystal reports, I can call either a view or stored procedure to pull back the data to my report. Is there a speed difference or a benefit of using one over the other?

A: Views are able to be pre-populated or scheduled so that there is no run time when Crystal calls it, otherwise, Crystal plugs into the view and the view has to run.

Stored Procedures are generally used to handle more complicated, accumulated data (like summarizing a bunch of different data). Crystal can call, as you say, as stored procedure, but it must wait for the stored procedure to run through its code and deliver back up the data for Crystal to display.

Another factor is that using a Stored Procedure (or a SQL Command Object, which is conceptually the same) will hinder you from efficiently using some Crystal Reports functionality.

As an example:

You have a report design requirement to have a single parameter that allows users to select one item, multiple items or all items. You can do this with Crystal Reports parameters in such a way that the criteria are always passed to the database for processing. Stored Procedure parameters, however, do not allow you to select an array (multiple) of parameter values. In order to provide the same functionality, you'd have to:

1. Create a single string-type parameter with user-delimited values and then parse out the values within the SQL itself. This is much more difficult than it needs to be....

2. Create a Crystal Reports parameter on top of the stored procedure. The problem is that this parameter will always be processed on the client instead of on the server when the stored procedure is executed (because the stored procedure has to be called before any Crystal functionality is allowed).

The result is slower processing, too much data being passed over the network and an inefficient report.

Unless you need to manipulate the data in a more advanced manner, views are typically better.

Ultimately, it comes down to what you are trying to do and what you need to handle for data. I know some CR developers only work with stored procedures but there is that trade off in having to call the SP and it does its magic. Whereas a view can be pre-populated or it can be a dynamic view which also has to run when it is called.

Always keep in mind how the CR engine plays with the underlying database query engine.

INDEX

www.ingramcontent.com/pod-product-compliance
Lightning Source LLC
Chambersburg PA
CBHW021050210326
41598CB00016B/1156

* 9 7 8 1 6 0 3 3 2 0 2 3 8 *